Designer: Elaine S. Furlow
Editorial Assistant: Myrna Adams West
Photographic Lab Technician: Paul Obregon
Artist: Debbie Petticord

Library of Congress Cataloging in Publication Data

Rutledge, Don
  The human touch.

  Includes index.
  1. Baptists—Missions. 2. Missionaries, American.
3. Missions, Home. I. Furlow, Elaine Selcraig,
1947- II. Title.
BV2520.R87   266'.6'1   75-2365

THE HUMAN TOUCH

Crossing Barriers
In National Missions

Photographed by Don Rutledge
Written by Elaine Selcraig Furlow

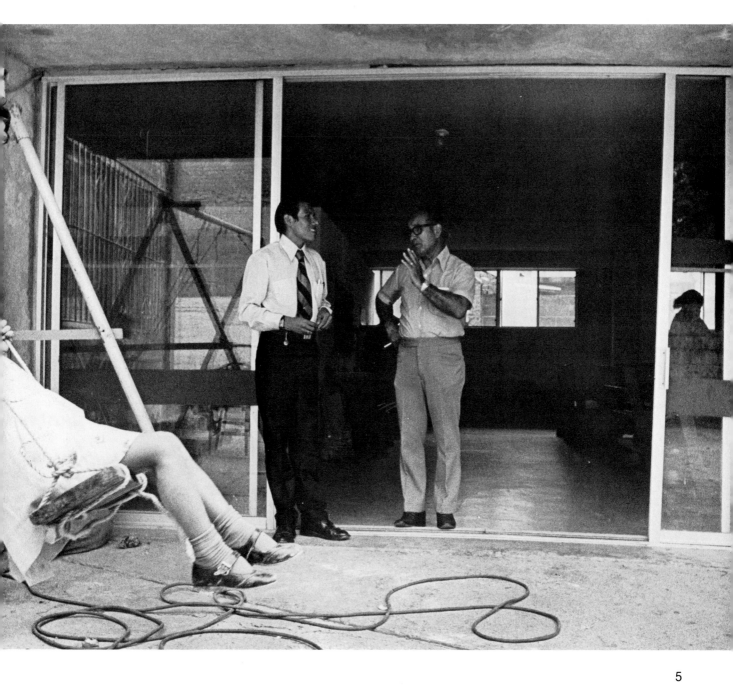

STEPPINGSTONES into Today's Complex Culture

Marie and Juan struggle with the dusty existence that characterizes life in the border town of Laredo, Texas. Billy walks the streets of Watts, somehow filling in the empty hours after high school and before sleep.

Isaac paces the corridors of Wall Street, looking for a financial kill or that big break which will mark success across his well-dressed shoulders.

Kikuo moves with easy grace between the surfing world of the beach and the intense pressure of modern urban life in Honolulu.

Mary Elizabeth reaches out from her isolation up Bear's Claw Creek to touch the gleaming promise of a larger world revealed by television.

Betty Hawthorne climbs the four flights with her inflation-lightened groceries to a tenement in inner city Worcester, Massachusetts.

Buck turns the pickup truck off the interstate for the long drive over the dirt road that cuts through the ranch and wheat land of central Kansas.

In human terms these persons are the "whosoever" of John's inviting gospel. They are a very important part of "all the world" of the great commission, the mission Christ urges all of us to be about. When feet are put to the "go" of that commission, where does one go? How do you respond to very difficult situations? How does one climb over the barriers represented in these situations and in these lives?

Can one person speak the Spanish necessary to communicate well in Laredo?

Can he also transcend the boredom and prejudice society compresses into Watts?

Can he speak to the symbols and the emotions of a strong traditional religion, einforced by family associations and customs?

Can he overcome the suspicions an isolated community has of strangers?

Can he have the time to travel the empty miles to visit the ranch or to walk the stairs to that dimly lighted corridor from which Mrs. Hawthorne enters her apartment?

How can we cross such barriers of language, race, culture, religion, economics and geography?

One way is to find someone who is on the other side of the barrier, for whom the barrier may not even exist, or whose energy, love and sense of God's call has led him or her to leap the barrier with the high-hurdle grace of an Olympic star. In other words, find the Mike Mojicas, the Glenn Haradas, the Henry Chiles, the Freeda Harrises, the Glenn Iglehearts, the Sid Smiths or Bob Tremaines. For them the barriers almost become stepping-stones into the lives of people like Marie, Billy, Isaac, Kikuo and others.

These are the barriers one leaps to bring reconciliation—to make friends. In Paul's words, "All this is done by God, who through Christ changed us from enemies into his friends, and gave us the task of making others his friends also. Our message is that God was making friends of all men through Christ." That's crossing the most important barrier of all—alienation. That alienation is often expressed between one person and another, and between persons and God.

Missionaries like Glenn and Freeda and Henry and Bob are in the friend-making business, and this book sets out to tell just that story—how these missionaries cross barriers to make disciples of Jesus Christ of persons, all kinds of persons. The divine intervention is actually in human terms, a very human touch.

Publishing a book with the focus on personalities runs the risk of leaving the impression that these missionaries are superstars winning the games almost singlehanded. Instead, they are only a few of the more than 2,000 missionaries under appointment by the Home Mission Board and the state Baptist conventions. The personalities of this book also are not above mistakes. They are flawed with the same clay as the rest of us. They struggle with frustration, failure.

These missionaries are doing effective work, but they also had to fit into a larger plan for the book. The editor struggled with presenting missionaries at work crossing the barriers in home missions, as well as missionaries who provide a mix as to personality, geography, sex, race and age. Mission leaders recommended more than 100 names, and from that long list, seven were selected for this book. That leaves unreported 2,000 or more with active, interesting ministries and lives.

Most who work at communications suffer from short deadlines, limited space and all too superficial contacts with those of whom we write. This book seeks to cross those barriers also, and it is the first of a series designed to report on all phases of home missions.

Photographer Don Rutledge and Journalist Elaine Furlow set out to capture visually and with words the lives of these missionaries—their environment, goals, problems, personalities and the people with whom they work. To produce this book they traveled thousands of miles, slept in crowded trailers and dusty motels. They skipped meals, had near-misses of flights, and occasionally pushed beyond the limits of wise endurance just to catch the right picture and the last details of an interview or incident.

Of course, it wasn't all sacrifice. They did visit Hawaii, roared through long, open spaces of the Dakotas, touched the wonder of a border town, and marveled at the tradition and static life of Appalachia. They made friends of some interesting persons.

Don and Elaine visited, more than once where possible, every one of the missionaries. They stayed long enough to report both the context in which the missionaries' work takes place and who they are. They discovered not only the "missionaries" but who they are as members of a family, of a community and as persons one would like to know.

These accounts allow the missionaries to transcend the pages and become persons of dimension and character, living in a real world filled with victories and failures, with sorrows and joys, with hopes and dreams, and with daily struggles over everything from leaking faucets to race riots.　　　　—*Walker L. Knight*

MOJICA

In the border town of Laredo, Garcias outnumber Smiths 2 to 1. Mike Mojica, a Mexican-American, moves freely in that culture.

On a spring morning, Laredo, Texas, wakes up like any other city but its people and pace are tinged by its location—sprawled along the Rio Grande, on the U.S.-Mexico border.

Downtown, the busboy at La Posada Hotel sweeps off the front sidewalk. On his way to work, a beige-uniformed official walks past San Agustin Square, to the immigration office at the International Bridge.

Three girls in grey plaid jumpers and white knee socks linger on the square before finally drifting off to parochial school. A block away, a knot of Mexican-American men talk by the taxicab stand.

By 8:30 A.M., the swarm of blue-jeaned youngsters at United Intermediate School has finally quieted down in the modular classrooms. When the public address system blares them to attention, they stand and recite the pledge of allegiance—first in English, then without a pause, in Spanish.

For Laredo is most of all a city per-

meated by the Spanish language and culture. About 80,000 people live here. Nearly 90 percent of them have a Mexican background. Stores have no need to put *"Se habla Español"* signs in their windows, for nearly everyone speaks Spanish.

In this border town, where the Garcias outnumber the Smiths by two to one, missionaries Mike and Betty Mojica move freely, comfortably. The faces, language and customs of the Mexican-American culture are all familiar to Mike. At church, the 54-year-old missionary sings the songs in the Spanish hymnal with seldom a glance at the book.

"Why not?" he shrugs, "I've been singing them since I was a boy."

Mike Mojica grew up in Uvalde, near San Antonio, and married Betty, a teacher, when she was a summer missionary in Texas. He spent eight years in the Rio Grande Valley as a missionary for the Texas Baptist Convention, and in 1971 came to Laredo with the Home Mission Board. His assignment: to help churches and missions extend their outreach, tell more people about Christ and show their concern through day-to-day ministries.

Mike's calling cards read: "Missionary to the Two Laredos." The companion cities of Laredo on the U.S. side and Nuevo Laredo on the Mexican side are linked by a heavily traveled stretch of concrete, the International Bridge.

The steady flow of people across the bridge—some 25 million each year— demonstrates the exchange of labor, goods and money. Hundreds of people cross to visit and some come to stay.

Nuevo Laredo, on the Mexican side, is a steppingstone.

"People in Mexico work to get the means to come across," explains Mike. "They hear, 'It's better leaving than it is to stay.' And they end up at the border."

Few of the immigrants come with the idea of staying all their lives. They may move on to San Antonio or Chicago, but they are still very much tied to Mexico. Even after they become citizens, visits, letters and language all bind them to home.

Mexico has infused the Rio Grande Valley with its people and language. But

Mike grew up as a Catholic in Uvalde. After his grandmother converted to the Baptist faith, the family slowly switched, too.

with the people come problems. Most cannot speak English. Many are poor and have few skills. They want their children to have "a better life," but must scrounge to provide for it.

The Santo Niño (Holy Child) neighborhood, on the eastern side of Laredo, is an example. The streets are unpaved, the frame houses are small. Though most of the people work hard, their money often

does not go far enough.

Far down the list of things their money must buy is medical and dental care. To help provide this, the Mojicas, working with volunteer dentists from the Baylor College of Dentistry in Dallas, set up free clinics in a white mobile van behind the Emmanuel Baptist Mission.

The mission is built of pine logs stained a dull pink. A couple of mesquite trees dot one side of the corner lot. A row of mailboxes, for the people who live on a side street, sits nearby.

Outside the mission a blackboard invites the curious in. Scrawled in chalk is "Pase a registras . . .", then in English below, "Come in and register for the free dental clinic."

A dozen youngsters and mothers wait on folding chairs in the hall, more play outside. Volunteers, most of them from First Baptist Church, which sponsors the mission, register each patient.

One girl who signed up has already gone home, and when her turn comes, Mike volunteers to go get her.

Mike's heavy-muscled arms wheel the pickup down a bumpy road to a small, brown-shingled house a few blocks away.

"Oh, this lady has such a lot of children," he sighs. "She's on welfare, I tell you she has a hard time of it."

Two faces peer from behind the screen door; three other children throw a scuffed volleyball back and forth in the yard.

In Spanish, Mike asks for the girl who needs to see the dentist. A sister and a neighbor accept his invitation to the clinic. Mike drives back to the mission, the pickup billowing dust.

The dentists have been working a week now. The white van's generator hums in the warm morning; a hand-lettered sign on the door warns, "Watch your head."

Though cramped for space, the three dentists, Roy York, Wuan Garcia and Vern Wood, work quickly and competently.

At one end, Garcia stands on the steps and calls loudly, "Sandra?" When a brown-eyed girl hops down the church steps to the van, he checks her name off the index card.

At one station, Roy York reports to a mother, "Okay," motioning to her five-year-old, "no cavities. Beautiful."

Vern Wood's voice comes from the other end: "Don't chew on this side today, stick to soft foods for a while, okay?"

Much of the work is filling cavities and pulling teeth, but with treatment come words of prevention.

"You've got a pretty smile," says Wood to a shy, brown-haired girl. "A 12-year-old doesn't need hurting teeth, do you? Now here's how you keep that smile. When you brush, get the upper teeth first, close to the gum, a couple at a time."

She nods, hops out of the chair and dashes down the steps.

"Most of the children are poor—they've not been to a dentist and do not have toothbrushes," Wood says. "But they don't have to spend money—they can use things like people used to; take a small branch, fray the ends and scrub with that. It's better than nothing."

First-timers are sometimes nervous patients. But the dentists are young, friendly and reassuring.

"We had a group of 12-year-old boys in here the other day," Wood says. "The principal brought them over from school. You could tell they were nervous, so we decided to bring the whole group in at one time. On the first patient we explained what we were doing and asked the other

kids to help us. That worked great—when the next one came up, he knew exactly what was going to happen."

"There's no trouble getting people to come," Mike explains. "We take handbills across the street to the school. That attracts a lot of kids."

Then Mike drives around the neighborhood with a loudspeaker on top of his car, urging people to drop by the free clinic at the mission. Friend tells friend and neighbor tells neighbor, and by the end of the week the dentists have seen more than 200 people.

"Sure, they ask us why we're doing this, especially why it's free," Mike says. "It's a tremendous opportunity to give witness."

The names on the cards are given to Sunday School workers in Laredo's Baptist churches and missions.

"We haven't had too much follow-up, and this is a weakness," Mike admits. "Pastors have been good about contacting

As a teenager, Mike wanted to be a science teacher. He was set to study for that in college, with a scholarship, when he "felt called to be a minister."

families, but they can only do so much."

The clinics, which rotate to various sections of town, have been operating since 1969. Two years ago, the Baylor Dental College in Dallas contracted with the state Baptist office to staff the clinics.

Several times, Mike has taken the clinic across the river. "The director of health in Nuevo Laredo was very strict with us the first time," he recalls. "Our dentists had to work under a dentist from there and they were closely supervised. But the second time, he said, 'Okay, go ahead. I know you, I know what you want to do.'"

Mobile medical clinics operate in much the same way as the dental clinics. Mike works through the Texas Baptist State Mission Commission to line up volunteers, then channels the clinics through local churches.

Mike's calling cards read "missionary to the two Laredos." He serves twin cities, Nuevo Laredo on the Mexican side, Laredo on the other.

With the help of pharmacist Raoul Martinez, the doctors who volunteer for the clinics can dispense medicine that Mike gets free from drug companies and Texas doctors.

"That reminds me," Mike breaks in, "I'm about out of vitamins. They need some across the river."

The needs are many on both sides of the river. In the Santo Niño neighborhood, for instance, an observer can tick off several. Katherine Clouse, a member of First Baptist Church, which sponsors Emmanuel mission, says, "We could use a well-baby clinic and nutrition classes. But there are only 600 Baptists in Laredo. We'd like to do a few things well instead of spreading ourselves too thin."

When Emmanuel mission was built three years ago, members of First Baptist wanted to begin some sort of weekday activity.

"We organized a sewing class—we thought that was what women in the neighborhood needed," says Mrs. Clouse, a trim, energetic worker.

"The Lord honored our faithfulness," she goes on, "but he didn't allow us to continue with much success. We were just going about it our own way, not considering which people the Lord wanted us to be ministering to.

"Then we prayed," she explains, "that God would send us the people that he wanted us to work with."

She put a small announcement in the Spanish section of Sunday's paper. It was simple—sewing classes would be held at the Baptist mission, 12 women could enroll by calling this number.

Within a few days, the class was filled with women from all sections of town. Mrs. Clouse and the other teachers, most of whom are from First Baptist, pick up the women and bring them to the large, airy room at Emmanuel mission. A short Bible study begins the Tuesday sessions, then the sewing starts.

Seven sewing machines ring the room. Patterns and still-to-be-finished dresses and pantsuits are stored carefully, tagged with each person's name.

Most of the women are bilingual, but they prefer Spanish. "The second year of the class, I ran across a county extension agent who had some printed instructions in Spanish. That was really a windfall," Mrs. Clouse smiles.

The first Christmas the class met, the women all wore their creations to a covered dish luncheon. "We usually have some 'event' like that so everybody can show off what they've made," says Mrs. Clouse.

Each of the students has been given a copy of Good News for Modern Man and The Living Bible in Spanish. Before the sewing begins, someone—often Mike— gives a short Bible study.

"At first the women came solely for the sewing," Mrs. Clouse believes, "but now they are coming for the Bible study, too.

"I think the personal application of the Bible is what they appreciate the most from the study," she continues. "They never heard about the woman of Samaria, for instance. They really enjoyed that story. We Baptists take the Bible so much for granted—this sort of thing makes you appreciate it all over again."

All the students are Catholics and the class sometimes raises questions.

One woman asked her priest, "Why don't we have Bible study?"

"That would just confuse you," he said. "Even I don't understand it all."

"Well, I understand it," she shot back.

Mrs. Clouse says emphatically, however, that the purpose of the class is not to take women away from their own churches.

"Some may, in time, believe differently, but we do not push that," she says. "Our purpose is to present Bible study.

"That's a little bit different concept of missions, but that's how we think we should approach it."

After Bible study, the hum of machines and voices fills the room.

Cecilia Lozana bends over her white pantsuit, carefully stitching an inset sleeve. Cecilia, who heard about the class from her employer, a member of First Baptist, says, "The Bible study has been a great benefit—learning about the life of Christ. Especially I enjoyed the miracles. Study has helped me deal with problems in the house or with the family."

Mrs. Clouse, a longtime Laredo resident, says many Catholics seem more open now to exchanging views and opinions than ever before.

"Doors have been opened here I've *never* seen in 30 years," she says.

One door, if still only slightly open, is to the youth of the Santo Niño neighborhood. The mission sponsors a Friday night coffeehouse, which draws from 15 to 40 teenagers. On a wooden platform outside a small, gray building in back, sandals tap time to the music and heads lift to inspect the occupants of every passing car. The dust occasionally whips into their eyes, but they keep singing, "He's Everything to Me," from the pocket songbooks.

One quiet, almost sullen girl sits on a blue bench; another sings lustily.

One of the teenagers, in a workshirt with an ecology flag sewn on back, tells of her work in the local Levi factory. "I'm the belt-loop kid," she giggles a bit self-consciously. "The next time you see the belt loop on your jeans, you'll think of me. I sew them on all day." For a week's work, she nets $63.

Another girl goes to school part-time, works the rest of the day in an office supply house. Some are finishing high school, but others long for the day when they will be old enough to drop out.

For tonight, though, they sing and joke in the dusk. As it gets darker, they sidestep the red ants and stickers and go inside for Bible study.

Ron Durham, a student in elementary education at Texas A&I, leads the study.

"Okay, Alfredo is going to read the Scripture about having faith the size of a grain of mustard seed."

A lanky, black-haired senior stands and reads, then Ron picks up. His voice drones on as Mike walks back down the hall.

"This really fills a void," Mike explains. "In this area, there is nil in the way of recreation, not even a park. What's going

on in there," he nods back toward the class, "is one chance for the kids to get together."

Alfredo and his mother, Isabella Ramon, often lead the coffeehouse studies themselves. His sisters Hortencia and Neomi come too.

"The Ramons, goodness," Mike sighs. "I don't know what we would do without this family, especially Mrs. Ramon. She will do everything for the mission. She is active in WMU, teaches a class, helps with the sewing group and fellowships for the kids . . . ." He shakes his head. "She's something."

The Ramon family is close-knit, proud, self-reliant. Mr. Ramon works all day and raises goats, chickens and pigeons in his backyard. Alfredo is the third male in the family with that name, and at home is known simply as "the third." He works as a grocery store checker in his high school's distributive education program, and won a Texas Baptist Convention scholarship to attend Howard Payne.

Ministries run the gamut: medicine for poor families who need it, Bible study for the mission's teenagers.

13

An older daughter is away at Baylor on a music scholarship; Hortencia and Neomi are taking guitar lessons at the mission.

The students in the class contribute 50 cents a week; Mike subsidizes the lessons. "I want to get some started on piano lessons, too — we need some music in the church," he says.

But the church has affected the Ramons' lives in more substantial ways. Sitting in her living room, the wind waving the patterned curtain behind her, Isabella Ramon talks about her involvement at the mission. When Mrs. Ramon is involved with church activities, she says, she is "muy contento" — very happy.

Three years ago, Emmanuel mission opened, and a friend invited Mrs. Ramon. Since then, the church "has helped me through difficult times."

"My older son fooled around with drugs, my husband was very sick, in the hospital three months; I was burdened down a great deal. The church was helpful to me then."

"I think the church needs much prayer, much spirit — people need to want to work, to do their part," she says, brushing back the hair from her eyes.

Mrs. Ramon is not ambitious for herself; most of her wishes are for her children. "I want them to be faithful Christians," she says. "If I could help them get started in their careers, whatever they choose, I want to do that."

Mike has known the Ramons since he moved to Laredo four years ago.

"We were cleaning up the house for the missionary, that's how we first came in contact with Mike," recalls Mrs. Ramon.

When Mike and Betty decided to become Home Mission Board missionaries in 1971, the head of the Language Missions Department, Oscar Romo, offered them a choice: San Francisco, New York, Puerto Rico, Laredo.

"I chose Laredo because, well, this is home," Mike says.

Fourteen years ago, when both Mike and Romo were with the Texas Baptist Convention, they surveyed the border area with Rudy Sanchez, an associate.

"We pinpointed 10 places that needed missionary work," Mike remembers.

Mike works with local pastors to expand their churches' concept of missions.

"When I came here in 1971, nothing had been done with those 10 places. The money and personnel hadn't been available."

The Emmanuel and Alto Loma missions have been started in the past three years, but "We need five more missions, right now," Mike says firmly. He drives around the familiar streets of Laredo, pointing out a site here, a needy neighborhood there.

"We need a mission here, between the creek and the expressway," he says. He points to a cluster of neat, well-kept apartments. They are somewhat old, but the grass is neatly trimmed and the window sills freshly painted.

But, he points out, "even if the Home Mission Board or some church said, 'Here's $50,000, build a new mission,' we would still be without the people to staff it. Personnel is a big problem. We have been looking for a pastor for the Emmanuel mission since October of 1973. I have just been filling in."

One solution to the problem is to develop lay leaders.

"That's how we hope to staff the missions," Mike says, "have leadership training and let those people gradually take over the responsibilities.

"Right now, my main concern is to get these men and women involved in activity and Bible study — then a building can come later."

Mike swings back toward town, stops suddenly when he sees a tent being raised on a vacant lot.

"Hey, what's that? We had a tent we

vere going to put up but we couldn't find
lot. I think I'll go see."

He U-turns and heads back to investi-
ate. After a few minutes' conversation
vith one of the workers, he reports eagerly,
Well, if they can put up a tent to sell
ires, then we should be able to put up
ne to sell the gospel.

"Lots of people would come to a tent
vhen they wouldn't come to a church
uilding," he explains. "Same with home
ellowships, Bible study in the home.

"Okay," he says, settling back in the
ar seat with satisfaction. "I'll remember
hat place, I'll work on that."

Mike has a way—sometimes moxie,
nostly persistence—of getting around
bstacles.

When Primera church, Nuevo
Laredo, needed new pews,
Mike heard of a Texas
church willing to donate
them. But how to get them
across the border? Inspectors are suspicious of any goods that might be sold;
the narrow streets around the church are
already clogged enough without a truck
being unloaded.

"You just get them down here, I'll get
them across," Mike promised.

He got permission to bring the pews,
loaded in one van and one trailer, late at
night when the traffic wasn't so heavy.

At midnight, Mike drove the trailer
across, past the checkpoint and safely to
the church. The next night, again at midnight, he started across with the van full
of pews.

This time an inspector stopped him.

"This is the second time you've done
this," he said suspiciously. "What are you
doing? What do you have in there?"

"Boy, I had a time," Mike laughs.
"Something like that happens and you
remember how carefully they watch—
they remember you."

Mike explained his purpose, got a
grudging okay, and maneuvered the van
down the narrow streets to the church.

It was at Primera, Nuevo Laredo, that
Mike met Roberto Saavedra, an energetic
man who lives with his family on the
banks of the Rio Grande.

The Saavedras' home is a small, open-
fronted hut fashioned from pieces of
cardboard, wood, time and chicken wire.

Their livelihood is casting plaster of paris
molds—frogs, bulls, figures—and painting
and selling them to curio shops.

It is not an easy life, and meals are often
meager. But Saavedra's grin comes easy
and often; his laughter spills over to children and neighbors. He enjoys his craft,
expertly filling the molds, shaking and
shifting the wet plaster to create the correct thickness of coating.

Saavedra seems eager to help his
neighbors, most of whom have immigrated
here from the interior of Mexico, often
Torreon. But most of all, he is eager to tell
them about Christ.

Through Saavedra's help Mike began
preaching at the riverfront on Friday
nights for a while. Eventually, he turned
it over to laypeople, and suggested that
Primera of Nuevo Laredo sponsor the
group. At the same time, Mike was teaching homiletics to 20 laypeople at Primera.

"This man, Roberto Saavedra, was the
best," Mike says proudly. "He was named
a missionary for the whole group by the
river."

One result of Saavedra's ministry has
been Hijinio Munoz, the most experienced
of the plaster mold makers, becoming a
Christian.

Munoz brought his family to Nuevo
Laredo from Torreon in June, 1972, "in
search of a better way. I had tried many
things, but I was without a purpose, moving place to place," he says.

Saavedra invited him to church. And
Munoz's bright smile widens as he
chuckles, remembering.

"They had a time with me. The first
time I went to church, I was drunk. On
the way to church I bought some chewing
gum so they couldn't tell my breath so
much.

"At the church at first I thought, well
this is just another religion. But when I
got out, I was thinking, no, this is something different."

He eventually became a Christian.

"The difference was that I understood
about the Lord and what I was able to do."

After Munoz became a Christian, he decided to teach his trade to others so that
the families by the river could increase
their income.

Friends scoffed at him. "Man, you're
crazy, they'll learn how to do that and
take all your business away from you."

continued on page 30

There are only 600
Baptists in Laredo.
"We'd like to do
a few things well
instead of spreading
ourselves too thin,"
says one member.

Through her seventh grade students, teacher Betty Mojica gains additional inroads and insights into the varied cultures of some of Laredo's families.

Mike meets all sorts of people
in all sorts of places—
a migrant worker in an
onion field gets the same
smile and handshake as
the owner of a gift shop does.

Texas church groups travel to Laredo every summer to conduct VBS and day camps. Children want to know why they come from so far away to do this. "It's a wonderful opportunity to answer."

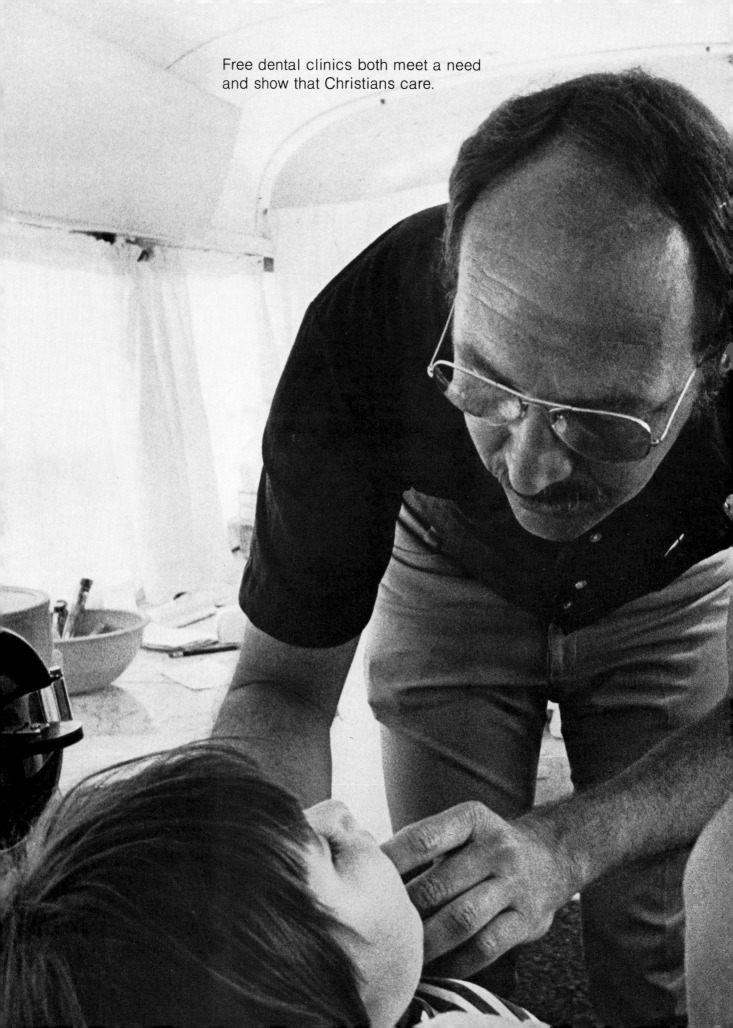

Free dental clinics both meet a need and show that Christians care.

Laredo's Baptist churches and missions
draw all sorts of people to all sorts
of activities — picnics, sewing classes,
worship services, even guitar lessons.

Life on the banks of the Rio Grande is not always easy. Mike's help is taken in the same spirit it is given—as a friend to a friend.

"They are a strong people," says Mike
of those who live by the river.
Roberto Saavedra and Hijinio Munoz
make their living by casting plaster
of paris molds and selling them
to curio shops. Mike helped
the two laymen begin a Baptist mission
among the riverfront families

Munoz answered without hesitation, "I have trusted the Lord for my soul, I will trust him in everything else."

He taught his craft to five other men, and soon his own business prospered. There was more work than Munoz could handle, even with the help of his two sons. The new workers were kept busy too, turning out *toros*. Because he taught his skill to others, five families had income when before they had none.

Munoz passes out tracts to most people he meets; he witnesses whenever he can. "Some will read the tracts and listen, some don't have such a favorable response." He shrugs, then smiles. "I keep passing them out."

Munoz himself has been challenged by acquaintances who question the validity of Christianity. The father of one of the little girls asked Munoz, "Have you seen this Christ? He's just a legend, just an old wives' tale." The man threatened to beat Munoz up, but he never did.

He refused to let his daughter go to church with the group until last spring, when Primera planned a special children's day.

"There were 70 children in the basement for the children's church and to break the *piñata*," Munoz says proudly. "We had 180 in Sunday School and 58 of them were from the river. That was a great day. There was so much joy in my heart I just couldn't contain it."

"You came to Nuevo Laredo looking for a better way," he's asked. "Do you think you've found it?"

"Money, you mean?" He shakes his head. "That depends. If the boys can make good use of their skills . . ."

He waves a hand at his wooden workbench, stacked with still-wet red bulls, and coated with small splotches of plaster. He will sell them to curio shops for eight pesos wholesale, about 64¢ each.

"The boys are doing okay, but it's hard.

"I know this, though," he adds firmly. "In other ways, it has made a difference, coming here. I have great joy now. It is my hope that all my children will become Christians, that I do not see them in the wrong road."

That's Mike's wish as well for the people by the river. As Saavedra and

Munoz began to trust Mike, he started helping the families with food, clothing and, occasionally, finding jobs.

"They are strong people, but sometimes it is so sad," Mike confides. "I brought over some Similac for the babies, and when I came back I found the adults were drinking it, too. They said, 'You know, Brother Mike, you mix this with chocolate, it doesn't taste so bad.'"

He delivered some medicine for children plagued with intestinal worms. "They had it so bad, that . . . do you have a strong stomach? . . . it caused those worms to come out both ends of the kids. They were vomiting and oh, it made you sick to see it."

His sympathy is not pity, however, nor does his help cause the river people to lose their self-respect. Help is taken in the same spirit it is given—as a friend to a friend.

Mike averages one trip a day across the river. As the blue pickup jounces down the Nuevo Laredo streets, he points out a few dreams.

"See that park?" A large expanse of green stretches from the river to a hospital up the hill.

"One day, when the powers-that-be will let us, I hope to have a service here in the park—wouldn't that be great?"

Many times, witnessing is simply a matter of seizing an opportunity.

"I know a woman who owns several

urio shops here," Mike says, "so one day I went to one of the shops and I noticed a Catholic Bible on the table. I just picked it up and started reading aloud. I asked her if she liked the Bible.

"'Do you read it all the time?' I asked."

"I try," she answered, "but I don't understand it all the time."

Mike then hurried to the Spanish Publishing House bookstore and bought a book of daily devotions and an illustrated New Testament.

"She was just thrilled with that New Testament," he recalls with a grin. "She didn't know anything like that existed.

"So doors are opening up," he continues. "It isn't just the people down by the river, but others also can be reached."

As proof, he points to the International Evangelism Congress last November. Thousands of people from both sides of the river came to the Nuevo Laredo stadium to hear speakers, then split up to witness to their neighbors. Mike helped coordinate the congress.

In 1973, there were more than 3,000 conversions in the border area among Spanish-speaking people, many of them in the Laredo area.

"Most of the people along the border are nominal Catholics," says Carlos Paredes of the Texas Baptist Evangelism Division. "They claim a religion, or a religion claims them, but they don't really have a relationship with Christ."

"Once a Mexican person makes a profession of faith, he will usually stick with it," Mike explains. "Sometimes still, the family will disown him, throw him out, but this is getting more liberal."

For several summers, Texas church groups have traveled south to help the Mojicas conduct Vacation Bible Schools and day camps along the border.

"We are beginning to make a dent in the minds of the people of Laredo because of the groups," Mike says. "Last summer we had 11 simultaneous VBSes in the city, and we got TV and radio coverage. I attribute the success very much to the groups who came in. People remember us because their kids are involved with VBS or day camp.

"The children want to know why people come from so far away to do this. It is a wonderful opportunity to answer."

Mike would like to see groups come during the spring and winter as well. "We could use help with building, repairing, visitation, everything."

One Texas pastor says, "I think sometimes it's a copout for the churches who go down there—they say, 'Let's go down to work in river ministry,' and they don't look around their own community to see what they can do there."

Nevertheless, Laredo needs all the help it can get. After four years there, though, Mike does see encouraging signs.

"The area around Emmanuel mission, the Santo Niño neighborhood—it's getting better all the time," he says. "See those brick homes? You're finding more of those now. The general economy is picking up."

The first year the Mojicas were in Laredo, Mike remembers many of the houses being boarded up. "Many of the people had migrated north to work the fields. Now there are fewer . . . I know of only a few from here."

San Agustin Square used to be filled in early mornings with men waiting for the trucks to take them to the fields. "But you don't see anybody waiting around here now because they have really cracked down on illegal immigrants," says one resident.

The border patrol recently returned 2,000 illegal immigrants in one month, compared to a normal rate of 1,000.

Nevertheless, some who do slip through end up as migrant farm workers.

On a hot spring morning, riding 15 miles outside town to the onion fields, Mike chuckles recalling an earlier telephone conversation. "When I called to see if they were working this field today, the lady said, 'No, no onions this year. It was a terrible crop. We don't have anybody working today.'

"See, I know her husband, but I don't know her, and she thought I was an inspector or somebody, posing, to try to catch some wetbacks."

He swings down a dusty farm road where workers are busy picking onions. Most of the cars and pickups parked there have Texas license plates, but now and then a Wisconsin or Idaho tag shows up.

Some leave in April, some in September. But the cycle nearly always causes some children to miss school. The gov-

Mike sees new needs every day, but says "the doors are opening up to all kinds of people."

ernment has set up a special school to help them catch up.

But some just drop out.

Rosalinda Martinez, 17, finished the seventh grade. Every day now, she pulls on her blue jeans and long-sleeved shirt, packs a sandwich, and rides to the fields with a friend.

Today she picks onions in the field near Laredo. Together, she and another girl can pick 120 bushels of onions a day. They chop off the roots and stems with shears, then toss the onions into burlap sacks.

They earn 25¢ a bushel.

"Today is not so bad because the wind is blowing," Rosalinda says. "Sometimes it is much worse, so we quit in the middle of the afternoon."

Her back still hurts though, from reaching over for the onions. And her gloved right hand, the one wielding the shears, grows layers of callouses.

Her parents picked crops, so she does, too. "It's not always bad," she says, brush-

ing the damp hair off her forehead with the glove. "My favorite is Colorado. The beets there, they are the easiest to pick."

Mike asks her where she lives, and when he finds her house is in the Santo Niño neighborhood, invites her to the mission.

A smile, some rapid conversation in Spanish, then goodbye. Not pushy, but genuinely friendly.

"I don't want to give the impression that we are only concerned about poor or hungry people," Mike says. "Other people sure need Christ, too. One of my goals is

to begin to reach people who are middl class or wealthy. They are a different sor of people than you see here, but the need Christ, too."

He recently gave the director of healt in Nuevo Laredo a *Living Bible* in Spanish and received a quick phone call in return

"I was nervous at first," Mike says. " didn't know what he wanted; I though maybe something was wrong.

"Then the health director said, 'You ar sure sharp.'

"'How's that?'

"'You know that book you gave me — that's what I needed, some spiritua strength for myself.'

"See, that's an opening," Mike goes on "We need to reach those kinds of peopl with the gospel, too . . . the people in authority, the people with money anc power."

He and Betty have tried to expand th concept of "missions" to all those they work with.

"Most of the people at Emmanuel thin missions is just the river ministry," explains Betty. "They have no concept o 'home missions' — it's just the river ministry or the whole world, there is no in between."

Before Mike and Betty Mojica came, there had been no HMB missionary in Laredo.

"The first year, some people asked me, 'Where is your church?'" Mike recalls. "Now they do regard me as their missionary. They like for me to report on other churches, what's going on. They feel a part of this."

Laredo has two Anglo churches, First Baptist and Heights. There is one Spanish church, Primera, and two missions — Alta Loma and Emmanuel. All are represented in the city missions committee, which meets monthly. "We coordinate things like the groups who come in the summer," says committee member Tom Forrest, an investigator with the Immigration Service.

"In the past two or three years I have seen more interest in missions. Building Emmanuel helped increase interest . . . our pastor (William Bolick, First Baptist) did a lot of work to prepare us for that.

"The thought is in the back of everybody's mind, to build more mission points when we can," says Forrest.

There are some 500 Spanish-speaking churches in Texas, with 43,000 members. Many Spanish Christians first became interested because of Anglo churches, such as First Baptist and Heights.

But Mike is quick to note that when an Anglo deals with the Hispanic culture, good intentions are not always enough.

"Sometimes a pastor will eat with the people, visit in their homes, get to know them. Then they get to a level of trust where he can do effective work.

"The person who is successful with Mexicans is the one who takes the time to get to know them as people.

"Somehow," Mike's hands turn, palms upward, "that person does a better job."

Although Mike does not say so, the most effective worker with Mexican-Americans is also the person who does not try to culturize as well as Christianize.

"There are different kinds of Mexican-Americans," says Carlos Paredes of the Texas Evangelism Division. "You have those who are completely Americanized, those who are in transition, bilingual and bicultural, and those who cling to the Mexican language and culture.

"You cannot try to change them, only understand them."

"In some areas of Texas, Spanish-speaking areas, they prefer English," Mike explains. "But not Laredo. Here, too many people have ties with Mexico. They prefer Spanish, so that's what we'll use at the mission.

"If we want to reach people, then we're going to use the language they prefer."

For the few people at Emmanuel mission who do not understand Spanish, the sermon is translated through earphones by member Tony Garcia.

Garcia, a short, energetic man who can preach as well as lead the singing, is a high school counselor. His wife teaches elementary school.

"Tony is the instrument of First Baptist getting involved in this mission," Mike says. "They moved here from Virginia several years ago, just because they felt the Lord wanted them to be involved in missions somehow.

"They are so faithful, my, if we had more like that . . ."

The mission does attract dedication, from people as different from each other as Faye Eutrell and Rosa Martinez.* Faye Eutrell is a nurse who teaches at Texas A&I. She has worked with Project Hope, and sailed on its medical ship around the world. She is young, committed, and will move on when her assignment here is finished.

Rosa Martinez is an illegal immigrant who is hiding with her three children until her husband, who fled north, can arrange for the family to stay legally. She has been here six years, speaks no English, stays inside most of the day. She sometimes irons for others to make money; her oldest son works for a bricklayer.

A year ago, Mike baptized her at Emmanuel mission. "God has helped me more since I've been in the mission than ever before," she says. "I wish I could learn more, get closer to God."

The brown-haired woman bends her head and fumbles with a button on her dress.

"And my children, I wish they could be in school and learn."

At first the children could not go to school because they were here illegally. Through Mike's efforts, they were finally admitted for a year.

"The younger boy, he's deaf," Mike says. "He came and made a profession one Sunday. I made a sign to him, did he understand what he was doing, did he want to be saved? He said yes."

Sometime later, Mike took the boy back to the earphones used for translating the services.

"I talked through them to see if he could hear anything at all, amplified. And his face just lit up. That makes me think he can hear a little, so I'm taking him to be examined, and maybe then . . ."

His voice trails off, picks up. "Do you have any idea how much a good hearing aid would cost? I wonder where I could get a good one for that boy."

If the boy does need a hearing aid, chances are that Mike Mojica will find one for him — somewhere, by some means. It seems a small thing, like the guitar lessons for Hortencia Ramon, the medicine for the families by the river. But the small things add up, and their sum is an indication of Mike's Christian concern for the people of the two Laredos. •

The human touch turns VBS from a "project" into a care-and-share time in a Laredo city park.

CHILES

Henry Chiles has updated the circuit rider idea, trading a horse for an air-conditioned car and travel trailer.

He and his wife, Bobbie, crisscross South Dakota to strengthen Southern Baptist work, especially through the state's pastors.

Henry's territory covers 77,047 square miles. The Missouri River, running wide and brown through the middle of South Dakota, splits the state into two near-equal sections. Baptists use the river to mark the boundary between East River association and West River.

Henry and Bobbie serve both, so they live near the center, in the capital, Pierre (Natives pronounce it "peer."). Home is on the third floor in a modern apartment building. "You get a little tired of carrying the groceries up and garbage down," laughs the 52-year-old missionary. "But with our schedule, it's better than having to worry with a house."

Last year they traveled more than 50,000 miles, rolling past large farms, flat

To overcome distance and isolation, Henry and Bobbie hook up the trailer and hit the road, visiting dozens of pastors, churches.

Bobbie puts in as many hours as Henry, talking and listening in relaxed, open South Dakota style.

wheat land and the rocky beauty of the Black Hills.

But the job is measured in more than miles.

When Henry took the job in 1972, Loyd Corder (the HMB's director of associational services) advised him: "Get the least amount of office space you can. Stay out of it as much as you can."

"He was saying I need to be with the people as much as possible," says Henry, "and this is what I try to do."

Being with the people is Henry's forte.

He was born with—or maybe picked up from his preacher father—a grace in greeting folks that would be the envy of an aspiring politician.

On first meeting, his handshake is quick, firm, his grin spontaneous. He will strike up a conversation with anyone— the gas station attendant, the man in the next trailer space. He has probably met 10,000 people in his lifetime, yet treats each with the same courtesy and concern.

His manner is that of a person who has stood in countless reception lines, listened to hundreds of life histories, remembered dozens of names and places and problems.

His dark, gray-edged hair is brushed back from his face. And a formal portrait captures a distinguished quality.

But the crinkly laugh lines betray him as a teller of tales, a teaser and joker.

"When it comes to matters pertaining to the kingdom, I refuse to argue," says Henry. "I debated four years in college, and enjoyed it, but I have won more argu-

ments here with laughter than with shouting and tempers. If I can get a fellow to laugh at his foibles, I think he's going to be a better person.

"I kid pastors, I kid Bobbie, too much I know," he admits. "But exaggeratedly, so they know I mean exactly the opposite. I express love in a backhanded way."

It is with this approach—at times lighthearted, at times serious—that Henry works with people.

Henry himself was a pastor for 30 years in Kentucky and Tennessee, so he knows from experience the problems and frustrations pastors face.

"My number one priority is leadership," Henry says firmly. "If a church has a good pastor, he'll get a building, one way or another. There is no point in putting in a building and saddling a church with a debt they can't pay, when they don't have a pastor to work to get the people."

To that end, he has concentrated much time and effort into recruiting capable pastors, supporting and encouraging them. And he gently guides their churches to give them the response—both financially and humanly—they need.

Frankly, in pioneer missions a few years ago, we used to get the rejects for pastors—the guys who couldn't cut it anyplace else," Henry says with a trace of regret. "The churches were so eager to get a man, they would jump too soon, sometimes. 'He wants to come so bad, he must be good,' they'd think.

"Now, that's not true. We are getting in a new crop of pastors. These men coming now could have a pastorate anywhere, but they are choosing to come here." He ticks off the names of several men—experienced graduates of Southern or Southwestern seminary.

The interest of young, untried pastors encourages Henry, too.

The youngest pastor in East River association is Glenn Ellis, a friendly, black-haired seminary student who drives 60 miles every weekend from Sioux Falls to the small town of Mitchell.

The Mitchell church—small, struggling, without a leader—had been looking for a pastor. Ellis, young but enthusiastic, had been eager to get into missions.

Henry brought the two together.

"He knew I had been thinking about whether to go to seminary or straight onto the field," Ellis recalls. "He threw out the suggestion that I go to the seminary in Sioux Falls and pastor the church here."

Ellis, 22, had been a member of Henry's Tennessee church. "He really preached missions," Ellis remembers. "He thought Paul was a super-missionary. I guess that is where I got fired up about the idea.

"I liked the personal contact with Henry. There was no pretense about him; he was concerned about you as a person."

"Henry has always been outgoing, a leader," says Carson-Newman college classmate, Warren Rust. "Back in school, we ministerial students would be sitting around planning street preaching meetings in the nearby towns. We'd just be talking, but Henry would be the one to say, 'Well, come on, boys, let's do it.'"

Rust, who also was a pastor in Knoxville at the same time Henry was, says, "He has that quality of rallying people around a good cause."

Henry's concern, and his ability to channel talent into needy areas, have helped several churches who teetered on the borderline of survival.

Sitting on the back porch of the Mitchell church building, he talks, nods, laughs and listens to Ellis.

"In Mitchell, there is a vacuum," Ellis observes. "Spiritual poverty. I don't say this bad-mouthing, but it's sort of like some churches say, 'Here's the gospel. Take it or leave it.'

"We want to be different. I think the people in this town used to be very leery of Southern Baptists, though," he goes on. "They didn't know who we were. Some of these feelings came from lack of knowledge. What you don't know, you're scared of.

"Now, this is not so. We have been taking the kids to camp, inviting families to Sunday School. Showing we care—that is how to correct wrong impressions."

If Ellis gets the people to church, though, he then must find the staff to take care of them.

"Lack of leaders—that's a problem," he says. "There's really nobody to teach the adult class but me. Then you can't pull good people out of the adult class to teach the kids because the adults need to learn.

The lack of leaders is common to several South Dakota churches. That prob-

lem and others get aired when pastors in an association talk together.

"You realize the guy up the street— that's 50 miles from you here—maybe has the same problem, or a situation he's overcome," Ellis says. "You realize the problem is not always local, personal, your own failing. We can exchange ideas on how to solve problems."

Henry also hears these problems of pastors and churches. His advice, usually given only when asked for, is honest and practical, based on long experience in the pastorate. "That's what's good about Henry," says Ellis. "He knows your personal frustrations. He has been there before."

In Mitchell, a very real problem was how much money to invest in the church's present building, a small, white frame structure, before looking for a new build-

Rural life and open road aren't new. Henry and Bobbie came from farming families, and have toured 49 states.

ing site, which the church could not afford.

"Henry's answer," Ellis remembers, "was to plan as if I were going to be here 10 years and spend money as if I were leaving tomorrow."

"In the meantime," Henry adds, "I will be looking for other places for support— churches in the South who want to take on a project someplace.

"The HMB says, 'Thou shall not solicit money,'" Henry says. "But," he adds, the brown eyes twinkling, "we just present the need and tell what's going on.

"Almost always, when I am answering a letter, I will start, 'In response to your request,'" Henry explains seriously. "People in the South have expressed interest. They have heard about pioneer missions and want to help. I just put them in touch with some church who needs them."

"Lots of people have connections," says the Home Mission Board's Loyd Corder. "But Henry's conviction, his manner and approach to using his connections is what makes the difference here."

The ties of the Chiles to churches in the South are strong because of their long years in Tennessee. In 1972, Henry and Bobbie gave up a successful pastorate at Central Baptist Church of Bearden in Knoxville to become missionaries in the pioneer area of South Dakota.

When the Chiles moved to South Dakota, some people thought they were regressing. "They thought we had left a good church to start all over again," says Chiles with a chuckle.

Tennessee friends would often ask solicitously, "Well, how are you making the adjustments?"

Henry laughs, "I was sort of puzzled by that. Finally so many people asked that I knew I was going to have to come up with an answer. So I finally said, 'Just *terrible*. If I knew what they were, then I would make them.'"

The questions kept coming. "Well, what do you do when it gets cold?"

Henry would reply somberly, "You know, we have heaters up here, yes we do. When it gets cold, we just turn them on." Then his face breaks into a smile.

"It's not *that* different here," he goes on. "People are people. We are doing the same thing here, maybe in a different way."

The wide open spaces, hours of travel and rural life are not new to Henry and Bobbie. Henry's father was a farmer as well as pastor. Bobbie's dad ran a large dairy farm in Tennessee.

When Henry and Bobbie married after college at Carson-Newman, they determined that their family would see as much of the U.S. as possible. "When we were traveling, even when the kids were little, we'd stop and look at the different crops," Bobbie says.

Henry and Bobbie and their two children visited every state but Alaska. "And I sure want to get there someday," Henry says wistfully.

Being with people is Henry's forte. He visits hundreds of them, yet treats each with courtesy and concern.

Henry first felt the strong tug to pioneer missions in 1959, on a trip to Billings, Montana. "The contrast between what they had and what we had was so glaring to me that it's been nagging at me ever since," he says. Soon afterward he challenged his Tennessee deacons to tithe him.

"Now," he says, smiling, "I have been known to take advantage of deacons, and so I started out saying, 'Do you fellows believe in tithing?'

"And they said, 'You know we all tithe.'

Then he told them plainly what he wanted to do: "Tithe me forevermore," he asked, "to do mission work in that time off."

They allowed him five weeks a year, apart from his vacation, and the Chiles family began making yearly trips to the Northern Plains.

When he returned from Billings that first time, Henry said, "I don't know when, but I'm going back there some day."

So Bobbie Chiles, who in 30 years of marriage has learned to read her husband well, wasn't surprised when they finally made the break.

"At first," she says, "we thought we could make it by ourselves, maybe after we retired. But then we figured that financially that wouldn't work. We decided to go through channels and see what would happen."

Leaders in the Northern Plains convention kept talking to the Chiles. When the position of associational director of missions came up, they offered it to Henry.

"They talked to us and we talked to the Home Mission Board," Bobbie remembers. "Our kids were grown, the church was doing well. It seemed like the time."

When Henry was interviewing for the job, he said he planned to use the trailer and take Bobbie with him.

"They thought it was a great idea. Then the first time they tried to call and couldn't find anybody home, some people suggested maybe I should leave her at home.

"But I'm not going to," he says firmly. His jaw clinches in the same way that it does when Henry is voicing strong opinions on liquor, the press or parents of Little Leaguers.

"Bobbie is real valuable. Often pastors' wives tell her things they would never tell me. They confide in her, and let me tell you, the things the pastor's wife worries about are the things the pastor worries about. Bobbie is real good with this."

"I always used to go on trips with Henry, to conventions and revivals and such, so traveling's not new," says Bobbie, a friendly, outgoing woman who spends some of her free hours on trips making afghans and doing needlework.

One of the first things I did when I moved here was change my car tags," says Chiles. "Then I promised myself I would never begin a sentence with 'back home.' I remember in Tennessee when all those folks from New Jersey moved in at Oakridge. They kept talking about back home in New Jersey. We all got real tired of it — 'If it is so great, why don't you go back there?'

"I don't want to come across that way to the people here. They resent it, and I don't blame them."

Chiles says that some South Dakota Baptists, especially those who have moved here from the South, get complexes. "In the South, they belonged to the biggest church in town and everybody knew who Southern Baptists were.

"Up here, we're small. A lot of people never heard of us. It's easy to get an inferiority complex all of a sudden."

Chiles tells worriers, "This is a growth pattern. It's okay to be little, when you're *new*." He hopes the growth will come primarily from natives of South Dakota, not from chasing dislocated Southern Baptists.

"The Huron church is nearly indige-

nous, for example. That's what we're after."

Huron is a town of about 6,000, in the east-central part of the state. A college, three meat-packing plants and shopping make it a busy hub for the area.

The Baptist church in Huron is nearly eight years old; the pastor has been there two years.

All types of people belong to the church: an executive vice-president of Northwestern Utilities Company, the head of the city sanitation department, one black family and partners of two racially mixed marriages. Most of the members are new Christians and new Baptists.

"Everybody in the church is from another denominational background but one other family and ours," says Earl Evans, the vigorous, eager-to-please young pastor. "When people here see the name Southern Baptist, they think of strong Bible study. That is what our members are most interested in, too.

"When it was 25 below last winter, we had more than 20 adults for Bible study."

The Huron church gave itself the nickname, "Little Church with the Big Heart." Its big heart, Evans explains, reaches out to all sorts of people.

Evans' method is just to be patient with people. He says, "I don't high-pressure them. Some things just won't work here."

In this part of the county, for instance, ranchers are oriented to Sunday work and 'til-dark weekday work. "You're just not going to get them to come in two, three times a week for training, so you have to find another way," he says.

There are other obstacles to attracting South Dakota natives, explains Henry.

"Most of the people have grown up in an atmosphere almost totally 'works' oriented. The Baptist concept of once saved, always saved is new.

Henry feels Southern Baptists are looked on somewhat as intruders. "People say, 'we don't need another denomination. Look at all the churches we have here.'"

Rather than answer them directly, Henry answers with a question. If the person is a farmer, for instance, he might ask, "What kind of tractor do you use? A John Deere? That old oil-burner, that two-cylinder sput-sput? I'm an In-

continued on page 56

Another day, another drive...the Chiles cross the big state, encouraging church growth. To overcome miles, some members even fly to meetings.

HURON
BAPTIST CHUR

Henry Chiles is liaison between Northern Plains convention personnel and pastors in the two South Dakota associations. More than that, he's a listening ear for pastors' problems and needs.

Woody Northcutt, student director at Brookings,
started from scratch, getting Henry's help
to borrow/raise money for this BSU center. He's
the kind of pastor Henry values. "He could go
back to Texas this quick," Henry says, "but he's
dedicated to this. So I'm committed to him."

STUDENT
MINISTRY

Affiliated with Northern Plains Baptist Convention
of S.B.C.

Woody Northcutt
University Minister

Henry's approach is sometimes lighthearted, sometimes serious. His advice is based on his own 30 years as a pastor. "That's what's good about Henry," says young friend and pastor, Glenn Ellis. "He's been there before."

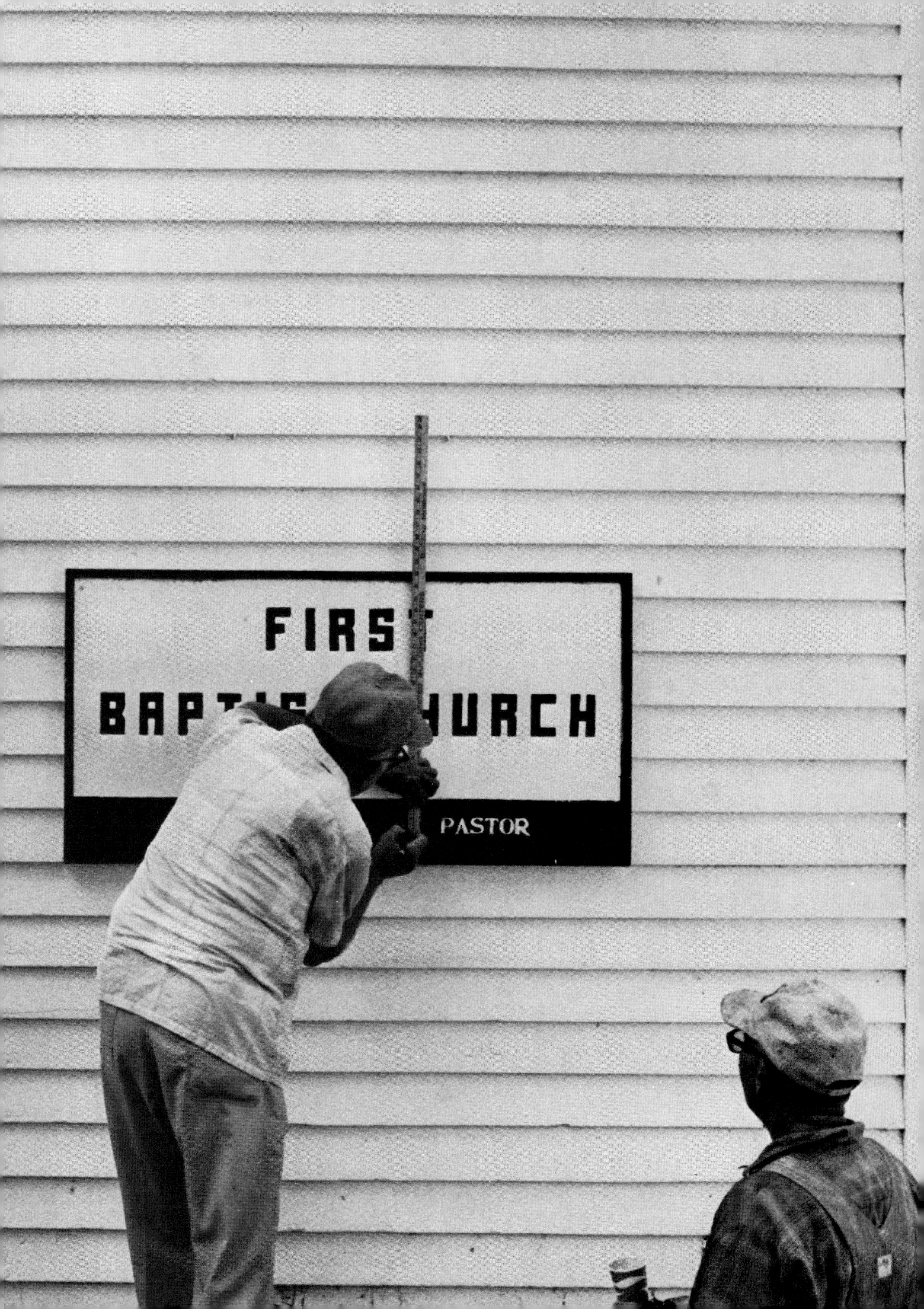
FIRST
PASTOR

The sounds of hammer and saw sometimes drowned out Bible stories when people from Central Baptist Church, Knoxville, helped the Bradley church repair its building and hold VBS. Henry puts such groups who want to help in touch with South Dakota churches who need it.

Missionary-pastor Ballard White faces the problems many pastors do—distance, long hours and limited resources—in his work with Sioux Indians in Eagle Butte.

VBS on the reservation is informal, free-wheeling, fun. "I like working with the Indian kids," says White. And Baptists from Far Hills church, Kettering, Ohio, who have come to help hold VBS, quickly agree.

55

ternational Harvester man myself. Why have a John Deere?''

Henry chuckles. "He gets the point. All farmers aren't alike; they should have a choice in equipment. Just like that, people should have a choice in churches.''

Evans says he "is just now finding some places in Huron that are open to me."

"There is a tendency to hold you at arm's length for a while to see what you're going to do," Henry adds. "If you read the minutes, you see why. One pastor was here for 18 months, another a year, then they just moved on.

"Now that's different. We have pastors who're going to stay a while and get some things done."

Henry observes that the pastors "get a little lonesome. They don't admit it, but they do. Our people don't complain, though, and I'm glad of it."

The pastors of the East River association meet in Huron each Christmas for their annual dinner. "Food's not real

South Dakota's farmers and ranchers put in a full day's work, going until dark and often on Sundays. So church meetings are geared to their schedules.

important, the fellowship is," says one. "We share, rejoice when good things happen to one another."

The association stretches from Webster to Yankton, about 200 miles. Evans attends all the associational meetings, even when they are in Pierre (113 miles away) or Sioux Falls (120).

The association's churches are still young: Henry wants them to avoid problems he's seen elsewhere.

"Where can you find an association that will say it has too many churches?" he asks, thinking especially of the South. "Where can you find people who will admit their failures? We need to admit that we could use some more intelligence in planning our churches—their locations, their relation to the community.

"Baptists say, 'I'm free. I'm free to do this or that or put my church here or whatever.' But I don't think anybody's completely free. We're only free within the limits of our responsibility to God.''

The associational missions director wants to avoid the problems that other, older states have encountered. But how?

"Educate," he responds firmly. "I'm going to preach fellowship at them [pastors] until they hate to see me coming. By fellowship, I mean more than the usual definition. I mean love that is a way of looking at people, overlooking differences, accepting people as they are. And I hope pastors hand this down to their people."

Nowhere is this openness and flexibility needed more than with the Indians of South Dakota. Nine Indian reservations are here; Baptists work in three of them.

Jack and Linda Coward work in northeastern South Dakota, reaching out to the townspeople of Bradley and Webster and to Indians in the reservation town of Sisseton. Henry visits them several times a year, to listen, observe and encourage.

Jack, a sandy-haired, soft-spoken pastor, drives his van on a Sunday route of about 140 miles to hold services in Bradley, Webster and Sisseton. He makes two weekday trips to Sisseton to pick up kids for his recreation program.

He drives, slowly, expectantly, through the housing section at the edge of town, glancing at the half-frame, half-brick houses to see if his basketball players will be coming out.

"There's Tim Goodbird, he's one of my star players." Coward honks, waves, motions Tim to the van.

Through such programs as recreation and the layette ministry for mothers of new babies, Coward has carved tentative footholds in the Indian community. Recently the Bureau of Indian Affairs asked his help with lodging when the Indian Women's Association met in Sisseton.

But, like most pastors in South Dakota,

Coward has neither the time nor money to do everything he would like to.

"We need to start with a young group of Indians and *build* up a group of Chrisians," Henry believes. "It would take 10 or 20 years, and there would be a high rate of attrition. We need to recognize this.

"I would dearly love to set up a day care center," he goes on. "Put in a kitchen and serve meals to people who wouldn't get good ones otherwise. We could do this sort of thing in a multipurpose building.

"But what we're talking about would take lots of money. And we'd need another couple in here, under Jack's direction.

"Jack has to look for alternatives," Henry says. "Since he doesn't have $75,000 for a building, a multipurpose building to start work with young Indians, then he does the next best thing — he lines up the armory."

But Coward credits Henry Chiles with being instrumental in getting some of the financial support the work in Sisseton needs. The van, for instance, was given by Florissant, Missouri, church.

And two years in a row, work crews from Central Baptist Church, Knoxville, Tennessee, have come to help the Bradley church paint, repair and renovate its building. Part of the visitors helped conduct VBS.

Outside the rambling, white frame church, the buzz of electric saws competes with "My Country Tis of Thee," sung lustily by the crowd of 25 at VBS.

The work crew repairs a stairway, removes a partition to make a fellowship hall, letters in the church sign with "Pastor, Jack Coward."

"When we first told the Bradley group these folks were coming, they didn't believe it," Henry says.

"Why would anybody come all that way to help paint the building?" they asked. They brought their ladders to the church, but didn't unload them, all the while suspecting the Tennessee group would not show up.

When they did arrive, only 30 minutes off schedule, the South Dakotans shook their heads, smiled and unloaded the ladders. Close ties developed between the two groups. The Tennesseeans stayed in motels, but two of the families often ate with Bradley families. They asked the Bradley group to visit them in Tennessee, and the next year, they did.

Such cooperation has contributed to the growth of the Bradley church, which three years ago was close to folding.

It was an American Baptist church, but when the town started losing population, the church lost support, too. The members had brought in Methodist and Lutheran pastors to try to keep the church going, but eventually, its doors closed.

Jack Coward went into the Bradley bank one day — "the only lively-looking place in town" — and asked if they knew of anyone who had attended the Baptist church. He then talked to Wilbur "Webb" Peterson and his wife, Doris, who eagerly accepted his offer to hold services.

Before Easter, 1973, Coward put an ad in the Clark (county seat) paper, announcing the service. On Easter, 36 people came — the highest attendance ever.

Now, though the church is unaffiliated with a denomination, it gives 10 percent of its receipts to the Cooperative Program, and most members subscribe to the *Rocky Mountain Baptist*.

Yet even with progress, Coward and other South Dakota pastors face problems.

"Being isolated, you miss the contact with other ministers," Coward says. "But it causes you to depend on lay leadership more and work to develop it. I try to train them, but so far there is not much response."

Henry has been working with those in the Northern Plains Baptist Convention office to provide more training for church members.

The Mississippi state convention has offered its help in setting up several sessions, which would give the widely-scattered Baptists a chance to grow and learn.

A major part of Henry's job is to encourage pastors in such training and to help them get the tools they need — literature, Bibles, vans, speakers, conferences, outside work crews.

HMB missionary-pastor Ballard White works with the Sioux Indians in Eagle Butte, a dusty patch of land just west of the Missouri River in central South Dakota. White credits Henry with lining up individuals to help pay fees for Indian youth to attend camp and arranging for a church to supply him with a van.

Henry's work varies — counseling one day, planning associational training sessions the next. But his purpose stays the same: to support, guide and encourage Baptist work in South Dakota.

White usually drives 2,500 miles a month, raising whirling, choking dust clouds on the unpaved roads. He holds four worship services — Sunday at La Plant and Eagle Butte, Tuesday at Green Grass, 20 miles north, then Thursday at a home for the aged in Eagle Butte.

"Denominations are not as important here," he explains. "Indians generally think all religions are good, so it is not as important to make a distinction as it is to teach the Bible. That doesn't mean I water down the doctrine, but we mainly stick to teaching the Bible."

Classes are often informal, freewheeling, but White builds on what is at hand. "If somebody brings in a snakeskin to class, like that boy did this morning, I try to build on that — talk about God and nature. We emphasize the Bible and a personal relationship to God.

"I like working with the Indian kids," he goes on. "Of course, we have our problems sometimes, but we just thank God for the years we've had here, and pray God will help us weather the years ahead.

"If the Indians didn't want missionaries here, they could have us out in a minute," White says, pushing his straw hat back on his head. "Course I hope they know who we are, and I think we have been here long enough that they know what we are trying to do."

One of Ballard and Bonita White's most visible ministries has been layettes for mothers of new babies. Churches and WMUs send gowns, diapers, undershirts, Bibles. The Whites give them to the Public Health Hospital on the reservation, which distributes them.

"Some of the women don't have husbands, some just don't prepare for the baby, and some don't have enough money to take care of the kids they have, let alone a new one," says White. "This gives them a start."

Along with the layette goes a letter from the Eagle Butte church, explaining why the layette is being given. "We often get calls from the ladies, thanking us," says Bonita White. "This is a point of contact."

Henry has arranged for outside church groups to help the Whites hold VBSes.

"As I interpret my job, it's to help these pastors, and I can't think of a better way than to get them in touch with group like this."

Last year, 16 youth groups and campe caravans worked in South Dakota.

"We get letters from people after they'v read something about South Dakota, but i really doesn't hit them between the eye until they come up here. That is one reasor we encourage the groups to come," echoe Bobbie Chiles.

VBS in Bear Creek, a small village o about 75, draws kids of all ages to study hear Bible stories, make kites and crafts

"I have noticed a difference this year i their attitude," White observes. "There i not as much interest in Bible school "This may be because of the unrest AIM [American Indian Movement] has stirrec up — some of them are more reluctant t participate in white man's activities.

"The Indians have to know and trus you as a person before you can do any thing," White emphasizes. "They ar somewhat distrustful — and they have right to be."

"Ballard has to walk a thin line," ob serves Henry. "He's a white man, but h can't be too much on one side or the other.

Says the missionary to the Indians "Some white man comes here fron Washington, stays a week, goes bacl thinking he knows all the answers. Ther they pass some policy.

"That is not understanding the situation. They should make a man live there 15 or 20 years, then he could understand the situation on the reservation and pass policies that were really useful."

An understanding of the Indian is jus as important in religion as in govern ment, White believes. "We got here 100 years too late," he says with regret. "The Indians got a mixture of paganism and so-called Christianity.

"It wasn't a personal, day-to-day kind of Christianity, though."

The day-to-day kind of Christianity the Whites want to teach is shown by the way they approach the people. When a young Indian girl tried to commit suicide, for instance, White went to the hospital, no knowing if she would talk to him or not.

"Finally she talked to me," he says softly. "She had just had enough, you know? She had several brothers and sisters. They had all ganged up on her and given her a bad time. She went inside to get her mother to help her, so they would eave her alone, and her mother told her to get out. I guess it was all too much. She mixed up all the old medicines she could find and took it.

"What can you say in a case like that?" he asks. "I said, 'Well, it may seem like no one loves you, but I care for you and I value you as a person. There are good things in life, even though sometimes it may not seem that way. You have many things I don't have—a heritage, for instance, and much pride in your culture.'"

"Pastors here are not climbing the ladder, not looking for glory," Henry observes. "They're dedicated to the job."

But even the most dedicated person can become lonely. "Sometimes you get blue," White admits. "Does anybody know or even care to know? It means a lot when Henry and Bobbie come by. Sometimes they are the only other Southern Baptists we will see."

"This is one ministry I can perform," Henry says, "to provide an ear."

As for church members around the state, they are not always sure what an associational missions director is supposed to do.

"People here often are not long-term Baptists," Henry says. "Some of them have been suspicious of me at first."

The Hereford church, in the ranch country about 50 miles from Rapid City, had been dead nearly two years. The remaining members were negotiating to lease the building to a farmer to store hay when they decided to make a go of it.

The church had a debt of several thousand dollars hanging over them and no permanent pastor to guide them. When Henry sat down with them to talk, he asked, "Would you like to consolidate these debts?"

"What do you want us to do?" they responded.

"This is just an option," he stressed. "I'm not a member here, I have no vote. You decide what you want to do."

Henry told the members he existed to serve them and help in any way he could.

"They have clocked in now that this is the way it is," Henry says. "Now they are warm, open, friendly. And they have gotten a pastor, so this helps."

The church constituted in spring, 1974, just after pastor Claude Francis, a retired military man, came. Francis, who was stationed at nearby Ellsworth AFB, said, "I wanted them to be self-supporting. I knew they could do it."

While situations such as the one in Hereford are encouraging, more than half the counties in South Dakota still have no Baptist church of any kind.

In a speech to West River association, Henry says, "I see two main tasks for us now. Seek to strengthen what we have and then lead in new work—outreach to new areas, establishing mission points. One and two can't be separated, though. They're like twins."

He goes on, "We need to redouble our efforts in every area, but especially in stewardship.

"What frustrates people more than anything is lack of funds," Henry says. "Not personally so much as for the work.

"When I ask pastors what their three most pressing needs are, I know what they will say. Money, money, money."

And he's right. The requests are specific: Claude Francis needs six sheets of plywood, six tables, 25 folding chairs for his Sunday School rooms. Ralph Ehren needs to buy radio time to start a weekday ministry in Rapid City. Lee Greer in Aberdeen has $20,000 in his building fund, but with rising land costs, he'll need to double that before he can think about starting to build.

Henry likes to tell the story of a friend of his who never could see the use of the Cooperative Program. "I could talk to him, tell him about pioneer missions, but I never got to first base," Henry says. "Finally I said, look, we're going back to South Dakota. Why don't you just come with us and spend a week there. I will just go about my work and you can see what there is to see."

The friend came, spent the week and got on the plane home a different man.

"He saw what we were trying to do," Henry says, "and that a lot of our money came through the Cooperative Program and Annie Armstrong."

Henry sinks back in the car seat, licking an Uncle Matt's Zesto sherbet, a favorite after-trip treat, and savoring the memory.

With a burst of energy, he starts the car and heads for the post office to pick up the week's mail. "Now if we could only get more people to realize what's happening up here," he says to himself. "If we could only get some more." •

"Sometimes you get blue," admits one pastor, feeling the isolation. "It means a lot when Henry and Bobbie come by."

HARADA

"Glenn, it's for you. Somebody needs a place to sleep."

The slim Hawaiian pads across the polished kitchen floor on bare feet and takes the phone from his wife, Roberta.

"Hello, yes. Where has he been staying?" The young social worker's voice comes over the phone in low, quiet, sure tones.

A few calls later, Glenn has lined up two possibilities, one of them a Salvation Army job training program which also provides housing.

Finally he himself talks to the young man the social worker had referred to. "Hello, this is Glenn Harada. Listen, I've got . . . either one of these places, yes . . . you can call them right now."

While Glenn talks, his dinner waits. And his bright blue fishing nets, still smelling of sand and salt water from this morning's expedition with some young people from a housing project, lie in the car trunk waiting to be cleaned.

The phone calls come often. Glenn sometimes refers his callers to an agency,

"Hang loose!" is Honolulu's motto. But the postcard exterior doesn't hide a big city's problems.

church or individual, sometimes handles the problem himself.

For in Honolulu, like any large city, people struggle daily with problems.

Two million people visit Hawaii each year—increasing numbers from Japan, and hundreds of American couples who buy matching splash-patterned aloha shirts and muumuus. Fresh off the five-hour flights from the mainland, not yet burned by the sun, they see for the most part a postcard version of Honolulu: Waikiki Beach, Punch Bowl national cemetery, Pearl Harbor, Pua Ualakaa Park.

The instamatics snap a surfer, a pineapple field, a hula dance staged by Kodak. The suitcases are stuffed with shell necklaces and monkeypod wood souvenirs. Then, carrying the specially-packed pineapples sold at the airport, the visitors board the plane for home or another island.

But Honolulu is much more than the crush of tourists deposited every day at the airport, and in many ways different

from the exotic, balmy picture imagined by mainlanders. It is more than the collection of high-rise hotels along Waikiki Beach, even though most schedules and shops are geared to the tourist in some form or another.

The islands, to which thousands escape looking for a change of pace or a better life, are part of the United States, but still isolated by 3,500 miles of Pacific Ocean— perhaps even greater distances in time, culture and tempo.

The "CBS Evening News" comes on TV at 6:30 A.M. the next morning; the "To-

day" show is really yesterday's. Almost everything but pineapples and sugar has to come from the mainland, so cars, housing, Cokes and clothes cost more.

About 700,000 people live in Honolulu, on the island of Oahu. Japanese represent about 27 percent of Oahu's population, Filipinos account for 10 percent, and Chinese, nearly 8 percent. Blacks, Latin Americans, Europeans and Polynesians are also sprinkled throughout the island.

Oahu means "the gathering place." A dozen cultures rub against each other with remarkably little friction. The edges have blurred, the distinctives between races have grown somewhat fuzzy. Yet social problems—many times similar to those frustrating mainlanders—persist.

To help deal with some of them, the Honolulu Baptist Association decided in 1972 to employ a Christian social worker.

It was a muggy June afternoon, Glenn Harada's next-to-last day in Louisville after finishing Southern seminary. Armed with a new M.R.E. degree, and a master's from the Kent School of Social Work, he and his wife, Roberta, were saying their good-byes to friends.

Then came a call from Edmond Walker, the executive secretary of the Hawaii Baptist Convention.

"Glenn," he said, "can you meet me at the airport? There's a job I want to talk to you about."

The job—director of Christian social ministries for Honolulu—was newly created. But the territory was familiar, for Glenn had spent six years in Honolulu: four at the University of Hawaii and two as a probation officer for the Family Court of Hawaii. He had grown up on nearby Kauai, an island about the same size as Oahu but much more agricultural and sparsely populated.

He attended the Buddhist temple as a child and fished with his Japanese father in the Pacific. Roberta came from the island of Maui, and for both, Hawaii was home.

"The job description sounded like it was written for me," Glenn remembers with a smile. "Put my social work background into a situation I was familiar with."

Roberta, a math major and computer programmer, recalls that at first she had trouble filling out the Home Mission Board personnel form.

"You know, the questions about when did I first hear the call and all that," she says. "Then I began to think of my role as supporting Glenn. I didn't have the same kind of training he did, but my role could be supportive."

Late in 1972, Glenn and Roberta were appointed by the Home Mission Board, in cooperation with the Honolulu Baptist Association, for a two-year pilot project.

"He's a local boy, that helps," says Soichi Tamura, chairman of the association's creative missions committee. "He didn't have to take the time to learn all the customs. We have all sorts of people here, you know, from the mainland, from the far east, local. They're all different, and he," Tamura thumbs over to Glenn, "has to make sense of it all."

Making sense of it all isn't easy, even for a hometown boy. But understanding the culture helps explain the context in which some problems arise.

"Some people in Hawaii are feeling trapped," he says. "It takes money to get here, but then many people don't have enough to get out.

"Hawaii has a high divorce rate. Intermarriage is happening more. An Oriental from stateside marries an Oriental from the islands, black-Japanese, Caucasian-Oriental, that sort of thing. Some people, especially parents, don't know how to handle the situation."

Other customs slowly shift as well.

"I grew up under a very strict family life," Glenn says softly, pushing the black-rimmed glasses back up his nose with his index finger. "My father worked, my mother was always at home. That's not always true for Japanese families anymore.

"You don't see the extended family — grandparents, aunts and uncles living in the house — like you used to."

Transition between generations is not always easy, especially for the Oriental who becomes a Christian. The concept of respect for elders is still strong, so many young Orientals do not want to antagonize their parents by being baptized. They'll just wait.

Backyard barbecues and aloha shirts in church symbolize the informal, casual pace of life for Honolulu's people.

"If we are Christians," Glenn says, posing a question, "what do we do when our Buddhist parents die? What do you do with the family shrine? There's a lot of tradition; memories of ancestors are tied up in the shrine."

The Haradas faced the dilemma personally two years ago when Roberta's grandmother died. The relatives all knew Roberta was a Christian, yet they expected her to offer incense and a prayer before the shrine, in the Buddhist tradition. To refuse would have shown great disrespect.

"We talked about it a long time," Glenn recalls. "We didn't want to hurt the family. Finally, Roberta burned the incense, out of respect for her grandmother. And then she prayed.

"But it was a very Christian prayer," he adds with a smile.

Both Glenn's parents are Buddhists. His father immigrated from Japan at 16 and worked on a sugar cane plantation on Kauai. While Glenn was growing up, he, too, worked the fields for $3.00 a day, and attended the Buddhist temple.

About the fourth grade, he met "Miss Grigg," a Christian missionary who worked close to his home. Her weekly Bible school was well-attended, he remembers, because "Being out there in the sticks, not having much to do, we all came to listen to her stories. She was a great storyteller."

Two older sisters and one older brother were later baptized in Honolulu. But when Glenn started to the University of Hawaii, he was not yet ready to become a Christian.

"I had gotten some bad ideas about Christians. One of my brothers who was a Christian would not attend my grandfather's funeral because the services were Buddhist. That was really painful for my father."

Another brother was so involved in church activities that he barely passed his university courses.

"I thought, if this is the kind of thing Christianity does to people, I don't need it," Glenn says, shaking his head.

When he did become a Christian later, his father's reaction was sympathetic. "My father's feeling, and this would be shared by many Japanese, is that if their child becomes a Christian, this is all right, because the child is still following some sort of religious life."

Later Glenn became involved in the Baptist Student Union and moved into the BSU dorm. Males lived on one side of the house, females in another. They shared cooking chores for the group and its houseparents.

"Glenn was my cooking partner, that's how we got to know each other," Roberta laughs. "Going shopping together with that little bit of money, trying to please everyone's tastes..."

After graduation, Glenn opted to work as a state probation officer for two years. Then came three years at Southern seminary and finally the phone call that led to his present job.

When Glenn returned to Honolulu, one of his first purchases was a 1970 census report, to help him evaluate the city's characteristics and needs.

"It's a fantastic tool," he says. "You can tell age groups, economics, everything. There was one Spanish area I didn't know about. Then Chinatown stuck out like a sore thumb—how poor it was, the levels of education. I knew it was bad, but not that bad."

Pinpointing the characteristics of each section made it easier to talk about how Christian social ministries (CSM) could meet some of the needs.

"My idea is for churches to take a more active role. They have moral leadership and resources—like their people and buildings.

"I'd like to tie every project into a church. I'll help any church get a project started, stay with it six months to help set it up. Make a base, cultivate it, then go."

In Chinatown, for instance, Glenn needs a church group to work with youth in the area's only community center, the "3rd Arm."

Chinatown, a sprawling collection of shops and small apartments, is backed against a new downtown shopping mall and bordered by Hotel Street, whose porno shops and movies are a favorite hangout for hustlers, hookers and sailors on leave.

Walking the sunny streets, where in mid-morning the pace seems slow and the conversations muted, Glenn points to a narrow building.

"That's the 3rd Arm," he says, gesturing to a doorway where several teen-agers stand talking. "They have some movies and a reading room, but not much money for anything else."

If a scheduled urban renewal project goes through, many of the buildings, including the 3rd Arm, would be leveled.

"We ought to get *something* going," Glenn says resolutely.

Although sometimes reserved and shy, Glenn can be persistent. He'll work through individuals and the creative missions committee to find a sponsor for the project and get it started.

The first few months on the job, Glenn struggled quietly to determine his role in

relation to the 10 churches of the Honolulu Baptist Association.

Some pastors thought he should be strictly a consultant. But that wasn't Glenn's or the creative missions committee's feeling about his task. After much talk the committee, which supervises Glenn, came up with four areas for him to concentrate on:

- consultation with pastors and churches when needed
- research on social problems
- model projects for churches
- Glenn's "own thing"—working with youth groups, teaching classes on human sexuality, or whatever he personally found challenging.

Cliff Hoff, pastor of University Baptist Church and associational moderator when Glenn came, says, "Our idea was to get a person who would be a coordinator. We pastors don't have time to keep up with everything—Glenn helps with that. Then he acts as an advisor on programs like our day center for senior citizens."

But some pastors felt they didn't need a Christian social worker's help.

"When I first came back, I was asked to speak at an associational meeting," Glenn recalls. "When I was through, one pastor came up and said, 'Glenn, you know me, you know my stance. And I know yours. Let's just work like we've been working.'

"I said okay. I've found it's better not to alienate people. Maybe later, when I am still maintaining the friendship, I can go back and try again."

That's typical of Glenn's quiet, non-pushy approach. "Perhaps that's because of my Oriental background," he smiles. "No, maybe that's a copout, I don't know. But if a pastor says no to an idea, then I say fine, let's just be friends."

He recalls discovering a church with a large number of divorced people. "I wanted to start a group there, maybe giving some help with the problems that caused the divorce, and other problems that the divorce caused. So I was talking to the pastor and he said flat no. He wouldn't even approach the people to see if they wanted it. I said, 'That's fine,' and we dropped it."

He shrugs, looking a bit perplexed.

Glenn's committee has encouraged him

to be more aggressive—a little less polite, a lot more forceful, in helping churches understand the needs and respond.

"That's one of Glenn's strengths," says committee chairman Tamura. "With the experience as a probation officer, he knows all sorts of agencies and what they are doing."

Glenn is on the mailing list of most community agencies, so if they have a

program, he can pass that information along to interested church members. Most of his contacts, though, come just through personal relationships.

If a Sunday School class wants to work with a similar age group, he can arrange something quickly. When a friend who is working to find foster homes tells Glenn the needs, he can arrange for her to present those in the state Baptist paper, so Hawaiian Baptists have a chance to get involved.

Just knowing who can do what is often a giant step toward helping someone in need.

Glenn does volunteer counseling through Hui Kokua (House of Help) at Kuhio Park Terrace, a high-rise for low-income families. Hui Kokua is sponsored by Methodists, but its director often refers people to Glenn for counseling.

"One lady from there called me early Sunday morning," he recalls. "She had just taken an overdose. 'My kids, I just

Harada, who used to be Buddhist, is uniquely suited to work in Hawaii's blend of multi-faith cultures.

continued on page 80

65

Oahu means "the gathering place." Dozens of cultures rub against each other here, with remarkably little friction.

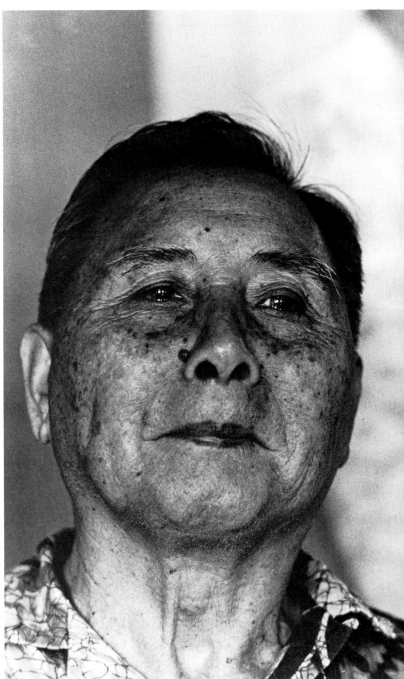

The islands are isolated from the mainland
by 3,500 miles of Pacific Ocean,
and differences in time, culture, tempo.
Yet crowding, poverty and personal frustrations
are as common here as in any American city.

Net fishing, diving and snorkeling
give Harada a contact point with kids.
He's set up several fishing trips
to get to know young people
from churches, schools and high-rises.

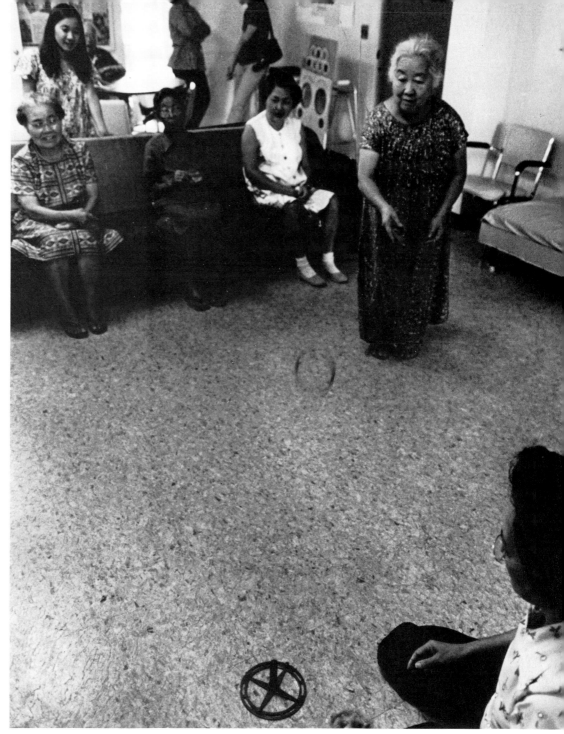

Through its day care center,
University Baptist Church opens
its arms to some of Honolulu's
older people. Fun, fulfillment,
friends—"This is the kind
of ministry I would like to see
more churches try," says Glenn,
a consultant for the center.

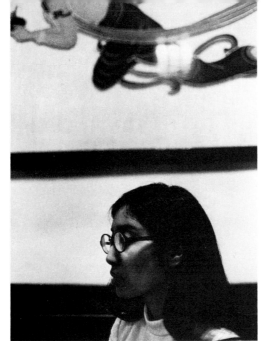

Harada seems at home in a variety of ministries — teaching courses in human sexuality, arranging a seminar on death and dying, helping churches set up programs, and just talking to kids.

Glenn works through individuals, churches and
his creative missions committee to begin
and encourage Christian social ministries.
And he thinks being involved in politics
is a possible avenue for even wider changes.

can't handle them,' she said. The frustration was too much.

"I don't enjoy the pain of counseling," Glenn says. "But I do enjoy helping people move toward a healthy feeling about themselves."

Through Hui Kokua, Glenn also began one of his long-time dreams, net fishing trips. Fishing, diving and snorkeling serve several purposes. It's fun, the novices learn a skill, and the lucky ones bring home fish for Saturday night dinner.

"I want to use fishing as a point of contact with the kids, to get to know them," says Glenn, a long-time fisherman himself.

The 31-year-old Hawaiian speaks softly, almost shyly. His approach—to kids on a fishing trip or to their mothers in the housing project—is low-key, unobtrusive, but sincere.

When he talks about young people, however, his voice picks up and the brown eyes sparkle.

"I don't know, I guess there is just within me a thing about working with youth." Honolulu is full of them—the median age on Oahu is 24.6 years old.

Glenn attends Olivet Baptist Church, where he teaches a class and coaches the basketball team. At lunch most weekdays, he plays pool and Ping Pong with the boys who hang around the church's rec room.

Most of them are from the University of Hawaii and Leaward Community College. "They're good, solid guys," Glenn says, as he bites into his hamburger and watches a teen-ager rack the balls at lunch. "That guy's a business major, the other one is in accounting. That guy shooting now—he's about to flunk out." Glenn shakes his head. "I don't know what's wrong, exactly —he is just having lots of trouble."

Friday nights, Glenn coaches the basketball team, which last year won the interchurch competition.

"Through basketball, I have developed a kinship with them," he says. "They are very free, very open, I like that."

O nly three boys on the team last year were Christians. "Some are trying to decide what the church is, what kind of place," Glenn says. Their relationships with Glenn may help them make that decision. They know Glenn is a minister, their Sunday School teacher and coach.

"Sometimes when I'm talking about Christian social ministries, I feel like a voice in the wilderness. Then there are people like Henry."

But most of all he is their friend—someone to talk to.

One boy on his team coached the junior team; three others were active in the city league. "I always encourage them to help other people—if they can do this sort of thing outside the church, just think what they could do inside."

The young people at Olivet asked him to teach a preparation for marriage class. "It was a sad thing when one of the girls broke off an engagement—partly as a result of attending the class—but she just had some questions about the relationship. It was a painful break, but better to happen now than later."

At another church, Glenn taught a course for adults in human sexuality. Members of the Aina Haina Baptist Church responded to Glenn so well when he was filling in for their pastor that they asked him back.

"Glenn has been able to do so much," says member Irene Honjo, "because he is a professional. In that class, for instance, the people respected what he had to say. They would listen."

When he started the class, Glenn was a bit doubtful about the reactions he would get. "I thought, 'Well, they will be a bit reticent, especially since they are Japanese.'

"The first question was, 'How do you revitalize your sex life in middle age?'

"Oh, boy," Glenn thought. And then laughed, "Roberta and I are not quite to that stage yet."

Other questions ranged from extramarial affairs to how to educate children about sex.

Glenn fielded them all with his Bible close at hand, atop a thick manila folder labeled "human sexuality."

The class was so well-received that the church's young people have asked for their own class.

Glenn has spoken at most of the churches in the association and knows all the pastors. "But I am an employee of the association, so an invitation needs to come from an individual church. I just can't go into a church and say, 'Look, you have this many senior citizens, this many people living alone—what about this project?'

"My social work orientation comes out. Well, each individual is an individual. I just let him be and move to an area where I can work."

Some people urge Glenn to be more forceful, but he thinks more people would resent that than be helped by it.

"When I started, I thought, 'If I can be the consciousness-raiser for churches—if they would think about what they could do, even if I'm not involved in the process of doing it, that's okay.' It's not necessary to establish a lot of projects to establish the validity of my position.

"But," he admits with a grin, "it is still hard, especially at first. The reality factor is sometimes hard to take. You come in with so many dreams.

"Last January I was feeling discouraged, and I wondered if the churches really wanted me. I knew most of them wanted me, but my question to them was, do you need me enough to use me?

"So many churches don't want to risk, but we have to risk to gain."

Friend and pastor Henry Webb says, "The good thing about Glenn is his development of the creative missions com-

mittee and the concept of Christian social ministries.

"One member of our church is on the committee—I think she's sort of caught the spirit and is spreading it to our people. That's a good way to work."

Webb has pastored Kalihi Baptist Church, on Honolulu's western side, for six years. Kalihi Valley is one-third Japanese, one-third Filipino and the rest a mixture of races and cultures. Twenty percent of the Filipinos in the U.S. live in Hawaii, and perhaps half of those have settled in this neighborhood. The Webbs are the only *haolie* (a word for a western Anglo foreigner) couple in the church.

"It's really amazing for a Caucasian to do what he's done, especially in this neighborhood," says Glenn. "It's a low-income area with lots of different groups. They don't think very highly of Caucasians.

"But Henry is easygoing; he listens," Glenn says. "He can go for 30 minutes without saying anything, and you feel he understands."

With Webb's leadership, the church has helped create a half-dozen ministries, including a clothes closet (wedged in a small room next to the choir loft), a medical-dental clinic and a team of community aides.

The community aides belong to the ethnic groups they work with. One aide speaks Chinese; one man's responsibility is the large Filipino population. The aides try to blanket the Kalihi Valley neighborhood, distributing clothes to those who need them and lining up people to visit the clinic. They pick up patients who need a ride and interpret when necessary.

The clinic, sponsored by Lutheran, Catholic, Methodist and Baptist churches, operates out of two surplus Navy vans. Medical personnel donate their time.

A 21-member board, which includes some church members, runs the clinic. "It's a private entity," Webb explains, "so the church doesn't have to worry with red tape and raising money.

"When we were talking about the need for a clinic, some questioned it," Webb recalls. "What does the church get out of this?" they asked.

As director of Christian social ministries, Harada wants churches to take a catalytic role in solving problems.

"When people ask, 'Isn't this a chance to witness?' I quickly say no," Henry explains. "We're not avoiding it, but this is not what this is for."

The clinic is there—the round steel supports of the vans slowly sinking into the church's paved parking lot—simply to meet a community need that individuals, business or government are not answering.

Projects like the clothes closet are the

kind that more churches can do, Glenn believes. "Not that much space or time is required.

"We need to develop centers, though," he adds, "so churches don't duplicate efforts." As an example, he points out that 15 churches contributed to Kalihi's closet last year—it's become an associational resource. When a flash flood hit the island's north shore in 1974, clothes were rushed to the victims.

"Sometimes when I'm talking about CSM I feel like a voice in the wilderness," says Glenn. "Then there are people like Henry."

Glenn thinks every CSM worker starting out needs a shoulder to cry on. "You want to cuss out the pastor, want to quit and get out. You need somebody to talk to." For Glenn, that person was friend and state hospital chaplain Kikuo Matsukawa. The two would get in the car

and "just ride sometimes, way outside Honolulu, talking about our frustrations."

To cheer up his discouraged friend, Matsukawa sometimes said, "Glenn, I've been working on a project four years, and only *now* am beginning to see results."

"I acknowledge that," Glenn says wryly, "but my gut feeling is that things *can* be done quickly."

Through Matsukawa, Glenn has started working a half-day a week at the state hospital outside Honolulu.

"Some patients here don't have any relatives at all," says Matsukawa. "And the adolescent ward—they could really use somebody. I know this is Glenn's area, his talent."

"I would like to see the churches taking turns," Glenn proposes, "one coming out for three months, maybe, then another church planning something for the next three months.

"Eventually there is the possibility of a church adopting a ward, and not just coming to the hospital, but bringing the patients to our homes and churches."

Glenn first plans a training session for the volunteers.

"You have to expect the unexpected," he smiles. "If you talk to a man who claims, 'I am Jesus,' for instance, how do you react? Many of the people have weird ideas about themselves."

Glenn worked in the outpatient clinic of a mental hospital for a while, so that sort of encounter is not as shocking as it once was. But it still disturbs him.

"It's been two years since I was out of that setting, so I'm still trying to clarify my own feelings," he says.

"I'm still a little afraid. But so many people need somebody, you just go ahead."

Recently Glenn came out of a committee meeting to hear that a man had jumped off the sixth floor of the building.

"In that same building were the Council of Churches, a society to minister to alcoholics, a suicide crisis center, the mental health office, Big Brothers, legal aid, credit counseling—and yet he jumped from *that* building."

People with needs don't always wear signs advertising those needs. Glenn is a volunteer for the crisis center, for instance, but so far only one person has called him.

In the meantime, Glenn has chosen a

more sweeping way to change the quality of life—politics.

He has written articles for the state Baptist paper—such as one alerting Christians to the upcoming issue of pari-mutuel gambling in Hawaii—and has joined a religious-oriented committee which studies political issues.

"I think so many things revolve around politics, you *have* to get involved. Government controls the lives of people. Christians have a very legitimate right to get involved." Glenn works on the legislative concerns committee of the Honolulu Council of Churches, which crystalizes issues, then tries to solicit opinion and fact, and make a stand.

"We feel it is necessary to address ourselves to the issue of creating a legal and social environment that protects and enhances the dignity, rights, privileges and services for individuals, children and families," begins one of the committee's position papers.

The committee has several special interests: family and youth, corrections, criminal law, housing, welfare, women's rights and the environment.

Anyone can testify before a legislative committee considering a bill.

"But it is so much better if an individual is part of a group," Glenn says. "You have much more impact that way, if they know you are speaking for X number of people."

Glenn has testified on a bill to make Kalaupapa, the leper colony on the island of Molokai, a national historic site. The bill recognizes the heritage of the people there and protects their privacy.

In another case, an area in the middle of Honolulu was slated to be zoned commercially. Glenn worked with others to encourage the state to make it a badly-needed park instead. The government finally earmarked $10 million to buy the land, so now a spot of green will be where a high-rise might have stood.

"Most politicians do want people to tell them what they think," Glenn says. "That's the tragedy of it. Nobody much takes advantage of it."

When Glenn returned to Honolulu two years ago, a social gambling law had just been passed.

"At the convention the next year, the first thing up was a resolution to complain about it. Well, that's too late. We're always Johnny-come-latelys. It is *very* difficult to get a bill repealed. The time to make your opinion heard is before the legislation ever gets voted on.

"Our people just *have* to learn what the process is, how it works and how to get involved."

Glenn's hope is to circulate information concerning the issues, have each church decide how it feels, then make a stand at the annual state convention. The opinion then would be relayed to the legislators.

"With my committee now, I have to make it clear that we are not speaking for every member of the committee, or every member of their churches. But if the Hawaii Baptist Convention could have every church member vote, then we would wield more power. Then I could say, 'The majority of the 12,000 members of our convention think this way.'"

Glenn has talked to a convention committee on issues such as pornography, environment and capital punishment. On any bill that concerns the convention, Glenn talks with executive secretary Edmond Walker. The convention is interested in a condominium project, for instance, so legislation on regulation/building of condominiums directly affects the convention.

The convention made a start toward involvement in 1973 when it voted to support campaign spending reform.

"It was a vaguely worded resolution, because it had been watered down to please everybody. But it was a start," Glenn says.

"When I started working on the legislative committee, many people were surprised that Baptists were involved in that sort of thing. Social agencies were a little suspicious, too—they're still waiting for us to prove ourselves."

Glenn knows he can't solve all the problems. "Man, it's overwhelming, isn't it," he says, looking at his city from atop Pua Ualakaa Park.

Maybe he can't even make a dent. But, working with churches and individuals, he's trying.

Half seriously, Glenn says, "Even if my position were to expire right now, I feel the churches have begun to get the vision of what they can—should—do. And that makes my time worthwhile enough." •

"I feel the churches have begun to get the vision of what they can—should—do. And that makes my time here worthwhile enough."

HARRIS

Mountain missionary
Freeda Harris directs
weekday ministries
in the small town
of Hellier, nestled
in the Kentucky hills.

Freeda Harris is a 60-year old mountain missionary. "I have few talents," she says, "But I can drive a truck. I told the Lord I could do that."

In fact, Freeda could make a good advertisement for a tire company: she has jolted several thousand miles on rough Appalachian roads, and had only one flat. And Freeda could make a good advertisement for vans: She's worn out four of them, carrying Kentucky youngsters from their homes in the hollows to the Baptist center, to study the Bible and enjoy recreation.

But Freeda, her wiry brown hair brushed away from her face, would disdain being an ad for anything.

"If you ever say something, don't say it about Freeda, say it about the Lord. We don't want glory for what we're doing."

Freeda, who was raised as a coal miner's daughter in Kentucky, stoutly insists that anything she's accomplished there has been the Lord's doing, not hers. She's been working there 26 years; at first unofficially,

Freeda, the daughter
of a coal miner,
loves and understands
those she works with.

then, since 1962, as director of weekday ministries for Marrowbone Baptist Center.

And Bob Jones, the Kentucky director of mountain missions, says that when he's talking about state missions, somebody invariably asks, "Do you know Freeda Harris?"

"You can tell she is well-known, well-respected in the area," says Betty Crow, who worked with Freeda as a summer missionary in 1972. It's sometimes said that a visitor can't find the center by asking for it, but can by asking for Freeda.

Making her rounds, she jolts in her white van up the roads to places with names such as Poor Bottom and Bowling Fork. Those are hollows—"hollers" to people who live there—valleys created from mountain creeks.

She picks up more than 125 mothers and children a week for the clubs and Bible study at Marrowbone Baptist Center.

You won't see Marrowbone on the map, but look close and you may find Hellier, a larger but still small neighboring town nestled in the hills. It's about 200 miles east of Lexington, in the wedge of eastern Kentucky that pokes between Virginia and West Virginia.

In the yards, yellow newspaper tubes for the Huntington, West Virginia, *Herald Dispatch*, are as common as those for any Kentucky newspapers. TV antennas poking through the trees can pick up stations from three states.

Hellier used to have a theater, bank, doctor, police department. That was in the '30s, when coal was king. The company store where Freeda clerked closed long ago, however, and the coke ovens that lined the hills are grown over with grass.

National energy problems have rekindled interest in searching out and mining pockets of coal. And today there are about 330 coal mines in eastern Kentucky.

Activity in the area has picked up. Not as many people are leaving these days, and some are moving in. A big highway is coming through Pikeville, the county seat 30 miles away, and new mobile homes move in by the day.

In the mid-'60s, dollars and strangers began flowing into Appalachia, the good intentions of federal government aiming to raise the economic level of the region.

While barefoot children and moonshine are no longer the norm, some in Appalachia live as they always have, alone and unconcerned. Abandoned cars are junked in the creeks, sewage treatment and garbage collection in towns like Hellier are still largely plans on paper.

Freeda sometimes puts on her rubber hip boots and picks trash out of the creek in front of her house, "but after a hard rain, it all just washes back down again. They dump so much in the creek."

Yet, nothing brings an angry glint to Freeda's eye quicker than an outsider criticizing her people.

"Everybody does *not* live in a shack with an outhouse. We still have some, of course, but look at all these new trailers—all this in just the last few years. Things are not as bad as some people paint."

About 914,200 Kentuckians live in central Appalachia, which includes most of the eastern third of Kentucky. Last September, 7.4 percent of these people were unemployed. The per capita income was less than $2,500.

It's hard to tell how many of these people live in Hellier, for the hills and hollows hide people, houses, trailers, roads.

Some are revealed only in winter when trees drop their leaves.

Close to 100 people a day come into the Hellier post office to pick up their mail each day. And nearly every family has members who come to weekday activities at the Baptist center.

Most of Hellier's people are proud, fiercely independent, bound by family ties and a tradition of clanishness. That atmosphere sometimes makes it hard for an outsider to work here, but perhaps it's part of the reason why Freeda Harris fits in so well.

As summer missionary Betty Crow observes, "Freeda has been there before. They respond well to her. She has the ability to put herself in their place and understand their problems."

Cora Fitch knows Freeda's concern first-hand.

Mrs. Fitch, a pleasant, roundfaced homemaker, has known Freeda 26 years. All nine of Mrs. Fitch's children attended clubs at the Baptist center, and that's how the two women met. Freeda invited Mrs. Fitch to the mother's club. She got involved in crocheting, sewing quilt tops, Bible study, fellowship—and eventually, Cora Fitch became a Christian. She joined the Baptist church three years ago.

Freeda hauls more kids in her nine-passenger van than it was designed to hold. Some of the children who rode in her van years ago have now grown to adulthood, with families of their own.

Petey and Betty Ratliff live with their daughter Melissa in a new mobile home off the main road. Petey's dad, a coal-miner for 47 years, lives in a small house behind them; he spends the sunny afternoons sitting on the porch, sometimes whittling, sometimes rocking quietly.

Petey Ratliff is a coal miner, too, and when he talks about his job, he shows a sort of studied indifference.

"It's not so bad. You get a pretty good pension—if you live that long.

"Somebody has to mine the coal." he shrugs. "If you're gonna eat, you've gotta work. Coal's about all that pays anything around here."

Ratliff, whose muscled arms bulge out of his T-shirt, was a truck miner for three years. He was a surface miner, working from the top of the mountain. Now he works for Bethlehem Steel, the country's largest employer, shoveling from a rib of underground coal.

With their new home, neatly trimmed front lawn, healthy family, the Ratliffs symbolize a bit of new prosperity in the area.

Betty Ratliff attends the mother's club now; someday her children will begin to ride with Freeda to the weekday children's activities.

Among her older friends, Freeda counts longtime resident Opal Birchfield, who has been here since the '30s.

Mrs. Birchfield has been the Hellier postmistress for nine years, running the

More than 100 youth and mothers come to the center each week to hear Freeda's earnest Bible studies.

flag up every morning, lighting the stove in the winter, cheerfully greeting those who come in for mail and stamps.

Mrs. Birchfield, a Kentucky veteran like Freeda, remembers when the company store opened next to the post office. And she remembers when it closed.

She's just moved the post office to a newer, larger building, and Hellier boasts, for the first time, a full-size sidewalk mailbox.

"I've worked hard all my life, and don't expect anything but hard work," Mrs. Birchfield says with a smile. "That's what

continued on page 104

Black nuggets, pulled from the earth, glisten
in the sun. In the coal-rich country
of eastern Kentucky, most of the economy and many
people's lives revolve around the industry.

Freeda grew up among the mountain people of Pike County, Kentucky. She knows nearly every face and name around Hellier; her simple, everyday concern touches people in every hollow.

Freeda's "people" are those such as the close-knit Stewart Baldridge family. Stewart works the 4-12 shift at a large coal mine. Sixth-grader Jody spends as much time on horseback as his mother, Spanky, will let him. Son Jackie is heading for college this fall; sophomore Paula is a budding pianist, and, with her family, is active in Freeda's weekday clubs.

Measured in miles, Freeda's rounds are not long, but they take hours of her time each week. She doesn't begrudge the time, but the 60-year-old missionary admits, "I'm getting weary in my body."

One of Freeda's happiest days was the dedication of the new Marrowbone Baptist Center last August. Friends and fellow workers in mountain missions gathered to rejoice over the long awaited building.

Many of the teenagers in Freeda's youth club
will go off to school or the big city.
But some will remain, eventually raising their
own families in Hellier, continuing the cycle.

Wednesday morning mother's club is an informal
time of Bible study, handcrafts and conversation.

our hope is, for what tomorrow is."

She nourishes that hope partly through the Baptist church a few blocks away, and especially through the Sunday School class, which Freeda teaches with vigor, enthusiasm and a simple stouthearted faith.

Nearby, Stewart Baldridge and his wife Spanky live in a neat yellow frame house in Cobb Hollow. Some call it Democrat Hollow—"That's all that lives here."

The Baldridges own land nearly to the top of the mountain.

Stewart Baldridge, a repairman in one of the larger coal mines, works the second shift, 4-12. Although the Baldridges live comfortably, they are well aware that coal affects their lives.

Before the United Mine Workers' strike last fall, for instance, Spanky Baldridge said with a touch of grimness, "Well, we've got a bull—we may have to butcher that. If they do strike, and you see the miners on TV, you'll know they are people like us."

People like us.

Spanky Baldridge, mother of three children, writes poetry in her spare time, spends much time with her family.

Jackie, a high school senior, is interested in the Air Force, and will participate in ROTC while he attends college. Paula

Simple, sincere faith is the cornerstone of Freeda's day-to-day life.

Baldridge, a freshman, and Jody, a sixth grader, are active in Freeda's youth clubs. Paula plays the piano—she takes lessons once a week; Jody sings often and well.

"About everything we do, we do as a family unit, "Mrs. Baldridge says. "One problem is all our problem. When I have a problem, I can talk to Paula. If she has a problem, she can talk to me."

Winters the family plays Monopoly and other indoor games. Christmas, 1973, Paula, Jody and Mrs. Baldridge cut the tree themselves, then dragged it home in the snow. "We looked like the Waltons," Jody giggles.

Spanky Baldridge met Freeda through her children, who met Freeda through the clubs.

"We have had a lot of prayer meetings in this truck," she says, referring to Freeda's white carryall.

"Freeda and I, everytime we get discouraged, we try to get together to pray. When we're too busy, we really miss it."

Jody's great loves in life are his horse, Pocahontas, and his singing, which he does at church and youth club.

"Jody, you want to lead one, honey?" Freeda asks in the afternoon meeting.

"Okay, 'Peace, Love, Joy.'"

The mostly-jean-clad group rises to sing, "I have peace, love, joy like a river...."

The voices are hesitant at first, wavering, but Freeda and Jody sing out, clapping, tapping their feet. A teenager in a plaid shirt picks up the beat, his voice getting stronger.

The concrete block building is less than a year old. Outside, its yellow paint still looks fresh; the grass planted last fall is just taking root. But the inside is beginning to look worn, and that's how Freeda likes it. For that means she's reaching people. All sorts of people.

Inside is a large room about 20' x 35', covered with heavy-duty yellow-green carpet. Bookshelves line one wall. A kitchen and bedroom are on one side; library and clothing distribution room are on the other.

Freeda usually picks up more than 20 young people for the Tuesday afternoon club.

"Oh, honey, this is not the half of them,"

she says, honking to call out another teenager.

Freeda has always encouraged her groups to remember the weeks of prayer for home and foreign missions.

"I know how much it means to churches." she says. "We take our pennies and nickels, and sometimes it doesn't amount to much, but you never know when somebody might have a hundred dollar bill." The group giggles, Freeda laughs and picks right up, "Doesn't anybody have a hundred dollar bill? Okay, now it's time for Bible study, does everybody have a Bible?"

Her left hand holds the Bible, outstretched, the right hand points and clinches. Freeda's voice occasionally trembles with emotion, but she's degrees more confident than the first time she did anything publicly in a church setting.

"I was 30 years old before I ever had a part in a WMU program," she recalls with a small chuckle. "I was scared, I trembled, I cried. I said, 'Don't give me another part.' But they gave me another, and another."

Freeda's parents came to Kentucky from Alabama in 1923. Her father was a miner, and when the veins in Pike County ran out, the family moved a few miles south to Harlan County, another coal area.

"Well, I was raised, I guess, in a home where the Lord was never mentioned," she says with sadness. "I'll not go into a lot of that. There are a lot of heartaches in my life I don't even like to talk about, but anyway, I was not ever told about the Lord. I didn't even know John 3:16 'til I was 30 years old."

Freeda was a beautician in Harlan County when a friend persuaded her to go to Sunday School. "I became convicted and gave my heart to the Lord." Freeda immediately got into WMU work.

"I didn't even know how God intended to evangelize the world. I didn't know he meant for missionaries to go. When we gave our offerings as we did, and sang that song. 'If you cannot cross the ocean and our mission lands explore, you can find the needy nearer, you can find them at your door.'"

This is the way it started. "I wanted people to know the one that I had never been told about or talked to about when I was a kid.

"Since I have become a Christian, honey, my faith has been strengthened time and again. If I had it easy, all the time, I wouldn't stay close to the Lord.

"When the devil tempts me," Freeda

Singing, talking, pushing, teasing, the children fill the van for the ride home.

says, "just telling me 'give up,' I take him back to Black Mountain and that little beauty shop where I accepted the gospel.

"The Lord led me back here to Hellier in 19 and 48."

Freeda committed herself to mission work. She supported herself by working in company stores around Hellier. She began conducting Sunday Schools in the hollows, and in 1962, was appointed by the Home Mission Board as director of weekday ministries at the Marrowbone Baptist Center.

"The most important thing is trying to reach people for Christ," Freeda says. "That's the whole purpose of my weekday ministries, to bring people into Sunday School, to get them involved.

"One of the little girls about 10 years old went up there one night. I just sort of thought how disappointed you are when you don't get others to go, and when we got home that night the mother came out to the car and she said, 'Freeda, I want you to come and get me Wednesday night. I have been so burdened.'

"I said, 'Now honey, if you are burdened, let's sit right here on the porch and let's have prayer together, all right?'

"Anyway, we started singing, 'What a Friend We Have In Jesus,' and she said, 'Miss Harris, the Lord has saved me now.' We all got on our knees and I wish you could have heard her praying. She was asking God to help her raise her children and that they might be saved too.

"She came for baptism Sunday night. Her son followed the Lord, her daughter followed the Lord, another daughter followed the Lord."

In 1972, Freeda rented a house on the hill for Sunday School. "When Betty Crow came I borrowed 5 little chairs from the Hellier Mission. We didn't have enough chairs then for everybody. So, when Betty came we prayed that the Lord would give us chairs, and I'll never forget that Sunday we prayed earnestly that the Lord would give us money to get the chairs.

"Saturday I went down to the center and Betty held up a letter and said, 'Are you ready for this?' It was a check for $200.00. I was speechless.

"Then she said, 'Wait just a minute, I have another one to show you.' Then she handed me another and it was $300.00. They were from her church. That's how we got our chairs and our curtains. It's still prayer, honey."

For many years, the center was in a two-story house close to the Marrowbone Baptist Church.

"It looked like a monstrosity from the outside," laughs summer missionary Betty Crow, "but the inside was fixed up real nice. We made new drapes that summer, with some money a church gave."

Freeda had her problems with the furnace. She had to stoke it repeatedly in winter to keep a fire going. And the old building wasn't exactly suited for several clubs a week.

So it was a happy day when Mrs. A.H. Jenkins of Elizabethtown, Kentucky, started a fund to build a brand-new center. She wanted to contribute to "a special project." The Kentucky WMU added $13,000 to that amount. The Home Mission Board contributed $10,250 toward the purchase of the lot, a few blocks away from the first center.

As usual, Freeda took a personal interest in the project. If lumber wasn't delivered in time, she drove into Pikeville to get it, hauling 2″ x 4's in the van.

Freeda has packed more than 35 children into her white, nine-passenger van. All she can see in the rear view mirror is heads.

"Oh, to Freeda this is the promised land," said a friend at the dedication of the new center last August. "When this is all over, she'll sit and cry. She's been too busy before now."

"Bro. Colvin [A.H. Colvin, state missions director] says the Lord has been kept busy answering my prayers, but he is not through yet," Freeda says. Right now she's praying for repairs on the van's broken horn.

Freeda sometimes packs as many as 35 youngsters in the nine-passenger carryall.

Singing, talking, pushing, teasing, they fill the three rows behind her, stacking up so all she sees in the rear view mirror is heads and hands. Several New Testaments fill the dashboard; Freeda's own well-thumbed black Bible rests there, too. As the van lurches up the rough mountain roads, the Bibles slide across the dashboard, the children bounce in the seats.

It is a familiar trip for Freeda; she knows where to watch for the soft shoulders, the best places to turn around and back up. The routine of jolting, stopping, rumbling up the roads and down again is a familiar one. But no newcomer can forget the experience, emotionally or physically.

Perched precariously on an inch of available seat, hemmed in on all sides by sweaty, shouting youngsters, conversation is in short snatches, if at all.

Freeda talks simultaneously to other cars and to the children piled in the van.

"Well, he's not giving a signal, I wonder . . . Hey, Mary, honey, we've been missing you. How're you doing, honey, your mamma feeling better?"

She grips the blue steering wheel, backs up, lets another child out. "All the fingers out of the way? You be careful, now honey.

"See all these trailers in here? These are all new, all new. These are the people with money, coal families, you can guess. Johnny, you getting off here or riding all the way to the top, honey?"

Freeda has torn out two manual transmissions. So her current van is an automatic. Despite the rugged roads, problems have been few: a blocked road one Halloween night, a flat with no spare back in the '60s.

"When I got back to church that time, the associational missionary was visiting in our Sunday night services and I told him, 'This is it. I'm not picking up any more kids.'"

Freeda changed her mind. Yet she still gets weary and sometimes worries about the future.

"I need a helper. It's going to take a young person with strength, industry. I don't want the work to die out.

"I hope to make it to 65. Course you never know. But I will always be working for the Lord. I'm getting weary in my body, you know you need some relief.

"I won't say I haven't wearied in the journey, but I've never wearied of the Lord." •

IGLEHEART

Glenn Igleheart is something of a religious middleman. The 43-year-old former Kentuckian is area director for interfaith witness in the Northeast. He explains Baptists to members of other faiths and explains other faiths to Baptists.

Americans are moving into a more complex, pluralistic religious society than ever before, and Glenn has a favorite story he uses to show that situation.

"When I was a kid growing up in Kentucky, our family got an ice cream freezer. You really felt big, being the only one with homemade ice cream.

"Well, for a long time, Christians have been saying, in effect, 'Nah, nah—I've got the ice cream, I've got the answer.'

"But now people are saying, 'So what? I've got some, too.'"

Glenn chuckles, and the gray eyes twinkle, but he is making a serious point.

"It's like being in an ice cream store, there are so many flavors of religion today. We can't afford to take the attitude, 'Look at me, I've got the answer.'"

"Interfaith witness is not picking a fight, but not avoiding controversy either. It's a middle ground— confidence in confrontation."

Glenn Igleheart's job is to be a bridge-builder instead of a wall-builder.

Most Baptists do believe they have the answer. Only trouble is, they share the world with millions of other people who are equally sure that they have the answer. Those answers may bear scant resemblance to the Baptist version. Baptists continue to believe the biblical admonition "Go ye therefore and teach all nations."

However, many of them, including Glenn Igleheart, believe the best way to do that is from a position of mutual understanding and respect.

One response in some locations might be, "We don't need interfaith witness; we're mostly Protestants here."

To that kind of comment, Glenn answers, "Do you have kids? Are they in the Army, in college? You *are* going to need this."

In today's "global village," next-door neighbors or the new face at work may have a name you can't pronounce and religious beliefs you know little about.

For example, Baptist Bill Townsend, who now lives in New Jersey, grew up in Little Rock and "knew probably three Jews, the ones I played football with."

"I didn't think of them as Jews," Townsend recalls of his boyhood. "They had Southern accents and all. I just thought of them as regular Southern guys."

When Townsend moved to New Jersey as an oil company executive, he found himself in a community that was about 30 percent Jewish. He began to get a better idea of "who the Jew is, what his customs are, how to relate to him.

"I wanted to be able to converse with them on their own terms, yet still bear a witness," he goes on.

That's part of the reason Townsend joined in when Glenn and several Jewish leaders set up a weekend conference among 10 Jewish couples and 10 Baptist couples.

They arrived Friday night at the Warwick, New York, retreat center and began with an observation of the Jewish sabbath.

Baptist Jane Medema remembers the candlelighting, songs, passing of spices. "This was all new to me—the reading of that scripture, 'How fragrant it is to have been with the Lord.'" In New Jersey, Mrs. Medema has more surface contact with Jews than she ever did growing up in Texas. Several of her son's classmates are Jews. Now it's not unusual to get an invitation to bar mitzvah. Mrs. Medema was unfamiliar with some Jewish customs and beliefs and was eager to learn.

The meeting began with discussions on Israel and Jews in the Soviet Union. Bible studies, with not more than 12 people in each group, filled most of Saturday.

Sunday morning, the Baptist worship service was based on scriptures from the Old Testament, and the special music had as its theme, "If with all your heart you truly seek me," from Isaiah. "We tried to plan around what we had in common," says Glenn.

"When we were studying the New Testament," Mrs. Medema recalls, "one Jewish man got hostile and said, 'Why do we have to study this?' A couple of Jews stuck up for us. They said, 'The Baptists listened to us when we studied the Old Testament. The least we can do is listen to them on the New Testament. We don't have to agree.'"

"It was a difficult weekend," says Harold Adler, director of the Anti-Defamation League of New Jersey.

"There were some stereotyped ideas. The Jews learned a great deal about Southern Baptists emotionally as each subject progressed over the weekend.

"The Southern Baptists were not prepared for the intensity of feeling of the Jews on Israel or the holocaust, for instance."

Mrs. Medema recalls statements about Jewish suffering in World War II, such as, "'If we allow the world to forget, another holocaust will occur.' They wanted so desperately for us to understand. They had causes they ached over.

"We'd say, 'We understand,'" Mrs. Medema recalls. "And they'd say, 'No you don't.'"

Tom Neumann, a Jewish participant recalls "raw emotion. You could hear voices trembling, comments like 'Whew, that was tough!'"

And both groups learned other, less emotion-charged lessons. "When we say, 'I've been saved,' we have a whole backlog of things to explain that—saved from what, how," Mrs. Medema says. "The Jews didn't know what we meant by things like that, so they reacted negatively to just the *way* we expressed our faith. That was something for me to learn."

Another sore spot for the Jews was the Southern Baptist idea of giving witness with a view toward conversion.

"There was an intense reaction against this," Adler says, "even after the reasons were explained. It's tough to have an acceptable relationship with a guy when you know he's not accepting you as you are, when you know in the back of his mind he's thinking, 'Ah-ha, I'm going to get you.'"

Townsend says, "I got a better idea of when and how to witness, when is the right time and when is not. I learned from that verse in Ephesians, 'Couch your words and phrase yourself.'"

Townsend's boss is a Jew, and they have worked together three years. "We had talked about theology before, but I think I'm able to communicate better with him now," Townsend says.

Despite some disagreements at the weekend conference, the groups didn't fall back into their own cliques like kids at a junior high dance. Coffeebreak fellowship and nighttime conversation were common.

Mrs. Medema says later, "I think the Jews envied us because we knew more scriptures. And some thought we were more articulate about expressing our faith. But that's just the tradition we came up in; we've done it many times."

A Jewish participant says, "It was not the areas of agreement or disagreement that were important, but the revelations about each other as Southern Baptists or Jews."

The weekend conference was a success, partly because participants were already interested in learning more about other faiths.

Harold Adler says, "We had specially selected people, and they were motivated to want to explore relationships. But no one walked away from that weekend as if it had never happened."

Rabbi Sol Bernards, who helped plan the weekend, says, "Well, you think about the amount of time, money and strength invested in that one weekend. So 20 families were touched, but it took so much energy to put that together. If these things could start spinning off, that would be better."

In a personal sense, there has been some spin-off from the weekend. Mrs. Medema,

"One religious barrier we have to cross is within ourselves, within the denomination. We need to get over our apathy."

for instance, who attends Union Theological Seminary in New York, chose to study Hebrew during a five-week intersession. "I want to understand the Old Testament better," she says.

"The Jewish heritage is part of our heritage. When we're talking about Buddhists, it's a whole different language and environment. But we share much in common with Judaism."

And the lessons learned have shown themselves in more subtle ways. Two weeks after the retreat, a group of Jews in South Orange, New Jersey, wanted Ken Medema, Jane's musician husband, to give a concert at a public school. They said he would be welcome to bring his albums to sell.

"We said, 'Wait a minute, do we have the right to sell records there just because we have the opportunity?'" Jane recalls. "We decided no.

"Ken said he would just sing about the way people related to one another—and not push the sale of his Christian religious music in a public school."

The Jewish women thought the Medemas were a bit eccentric not to sell Christian materials when they had the chance. But several phoned later to thank them for not taking advantage of the situation.

"I think this was our first time to con-

sciously protect the rights of people in the school," Jane says.

Mission study books do help Baptists learn about other people, she goes on, "but they can't change your life like that weekend did. There's nothing like becoming immersed in it."

Glenn agrees, but he also cautions, "The best kind of research is firsthand but you can't assume that what one Hindu believes is what all Hindus believe."

He stresses that Baptists who study any particular religious group still need to remain open, seeking new information and insight.

He knows he and the other three interfaith witness area directors can't teach every Baptist how to relate to every other faith. However, there is a way to multiply their efforts.

When Glenn talks about the hours of his job, they break down into "x hours with Roman Catholics, x hours with Jehovah's witnesses, but many, many hours training people how to do what I do, in their own situation, on their own level."

Glenn's territory, for instance, covers 16 states. For example, he did an orientation for summer missionaries serving in New York last year. The Home Mission Board's new US-2ers heard Glenn speak on the various religions and cults they might encounter; Journeymen, the Foreign Mission Board's counterpart, also got an orientation from Glenn.

He was keynote speaker at an ecumenical conference in Virginia and helped set up conferences last spring to teach Washington, D.C., area Baptists what Mormons believe.

Sam Simpson's Baptist church in the Bronx attracts many nurses; Glenn spoke to them about bearing their own witness while still understanding the religious faith of Jews and Catholics who were facing death.

At the old site of the Westchester Baptist Church in New York, about 200 Japanese were living in apartments within a block. Glenn held a conference on Japanese religions at the church.

He has been to about half the churches in the Metropolitan New York Baptist Association, and in April, 1973, he held

Glenn faces differences between faiths realistically. "I care enough about this relationship to go to a deep level and find out what you think."

three associational clinics on interfaith witness. About 50 people attended each conference, getting six hours training on the beliefs of Catholics, Jews, Jehovah's witnesses and internationals.

How do they learn? Through reading, listening, talking, role-playing.

He asked the questions, "If you were sitting next to a Catholic or Jehovah's witness on a plane, what things would you have in common? What would you know about this person's beliefs? What would you talk about?"

It's impossible to give a complete run-down on another religion when you're just allotted a certain number of hours.

Glenn gets frustrated when churches ask him to "come to our church and speak on world religions. You have 35 minutes."

He says, "I understand that you now can take a plane ride and in an hour cover the same path the Israelites did in their 40-year wanderings. That's a little bit like I feel.

"You can't tell a WMU group everything about Judaism in an hour, but you can get across a few main ideas," Glenn says. "Then put a disclaimer on it. There are other things about this religion—this is just a part."

World religions weren't always Glenn's main interests. As a sophomore at Murray State College in Kentucky, he wanted to go into politics. But during a youth revival later, he "came to feel that God was saying 'preach my word.'" During pastorates in Louisville, Glenn felt committed to the urban scene.

When the opportunity came to work in the New York City area, Glenn jumped. He was not really looking for the interfaith witness job, but "the more we thought about it, the more we liked it."

Glenn's wife, Nancye, is not an appointed missionary, but contributes in many ways to her family, church and community.

She is a deacon and state Missions Friends director. She helps with a Girl Scout troop, the school library and lunch program. And she has contributed in ways tangible and intangible to Glenn's new ministry in interfaith witness.

Glenn believes "preach my word" can be done in many different ways. "I don't think because I've left the pastorate, I've left the ministry.

"I'm convinced—if the gospel can't make it in the city, it's not worth selling."

In moving to the Northeast, Glenn had the joy of being on a frontier—he was the first interfaith witness regional representative—and had the freedom to write his own job description.

"Our department's philosophy is 'Put a competent person on the field, let him determine his own goals, and then live with them.' There is no checkpoint, but that's sort of scary, too."

The goal Glenn works toward is a situation in which individual Baptists, working in individual churches, can have faith and feel secure enough to bear witness to the person next door.

Security comes partly through knowledge and understanding. To build that security in himself, Glenn took a sabbatical last spring at the Center for Study of World Religions at Harvard.

Stacks of new books and a heavy schedule of classes were stimulating enough in themselves, but Glenn also was excited by the interplay of ideas. "I could hear people whose books I'd read or listen to some fellow I'd never heard of."

Part of Glenn's job is like a consumer's report—telling Baptists what's for sale, who's buying and why—religion-wise.

continued on page 128

113

On sabbatical at the Center for Study
of World Religions, at Harvard,
Glenn learned from class participation,
individual study and talks with
his six Jesuit roommates.
"One of the things I have been most
impressed with at Harvard,"
he jokes, "is my ignorance."

The interplay of ideas at Harvard excited
Glenn. His classes were on Islam,
Buddhism and Jewish mysticism, but books,
people and events of many faiths drew
his interest. "I'm looking for better ways
to do the job I'm doing," he says.

116

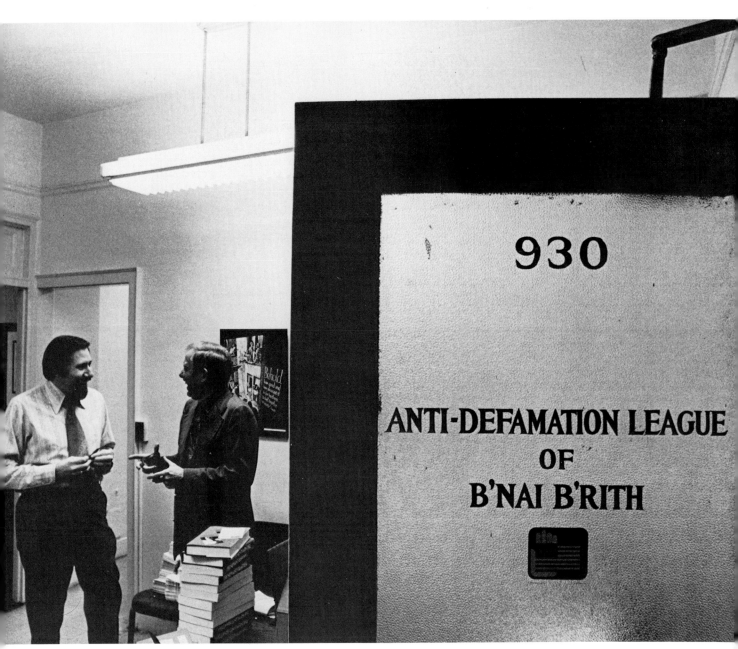

930

ANTI-DEFAMATION LEAGUE
OF
B'NAI B'RITH

Glenn learns about other
faiths firsthand by
reading, talking,
visiting, experiencing.
Then he trains others
"how to do what I do,
in their own situation,
on their own level."

The Iglehearts have busy schedules. Nancye is a
deacon, helps with Girl Scouts and is state Mission
Friends director. Glenn travels a lot through
his 16-state territory. But both Glenn
and Nancye find time to spend with their
two children, friends and neighbors.

Punctuating his sentences with energetic hand motions, Glenn tells listeners, "you can't pigeonhole members of other faiths." Glenn's calendar is filled with speaking and seminar engagements.

"Witnessing is a two-way conversation, a matter of seeing people, not labels," Glenn tells pastors, homemakers and student ministers in his interfaith witness class.

1. Interpersonal
2. Content
3. Programs
4. Teaching Skills

Interfaith witness associates are trained to teach other Baptists about a certain religious faith. Seven attended the first class, a weekend seminar on Mormons. They role-played encounters with Mormons, studied Mormon beliefs and looked up Bible references.

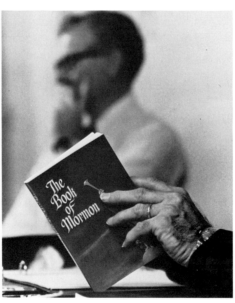

A Korean zen master was a 10-minute walk away. A crowded, paper-covered bulletin board advertised, "Trust in God, She Cares," next to notices for films like *Sri Chinmoy,* a movie about Hindu evangelism in America, or *Sunseed,* a documentary about communes.

Glenn gulped in as much as he could: one "name" speaker a week and films, plus his usual studies, classes such as Essentials of Islam, History of Buddhism and Jewish Mysticism.

"One of the things I have been most impressed with at Harvard is my ignorance," Glenn laughs. He adjusts a black fur cap, tugs on his gloves and jauntily sets off down the Cambridge sidewalk, watching the crocuses making a futile attempt to survive a late snow.

The scene is far different from Southern seminary, which Glenn attended in the late 1950s, receiving a B.D. and Th.D. He didn't have any academic background in world religions, but he did have enough energy and enthusiasm to match the new opportunity that came in 1968.

Since he was appointed to the interfaith witness job, Glenn has learned quickly — reading, talking, listening. And his sabbatical semester as a 43-year-old Harvard student was no exception. Despite the school's reputation, Glenn was not overawed.

He held his own, his mind taking in new facts and insights, his left-handed scrawl filling page after page in his green class notebook.

Although Glenn's classes helped him appreciate and understand other religions, he learned nearly as much from his roommates.

In his New Jersey home, Glenn had been eating dinner with wife Nancye and his two kids, Kaye and Kent. At Harvard, he sat around the table with six Jesuit priests.

He and the Jesuits lived in a three-story gray house on a corner of Massachusetts Avenue, three blocks from Harvard Square.

Glenn had trouble finding a place to live at first, but a Catholic friend arranged space in the Jesuit house.

They assigned Glenn an upstairs bedroom nook and quickly accepted him into the routine of the house.

Dinner was at 6:00; they watched the news together at 7:00. Then the residents scattered, to read, teach a class, listen to the BBC on shortwave radio or just talk.

Paintings by Father Dick Rousseau, a resident, hung on several walls. The Oxford dictionary rested in a place of honor in the dining room, for games such as guessing word derivations were as common as reading the *Boston Globe* at breakfast.

"The men at the house wondered about me at first — they may still wonder about me," Glenn laughs. "But we've had some good talks. Sometimes I interpreted for them: the things Baptists think everybody understands — like 'once saved, always saved' — they've never heard of."

"He did not come on strong with a lot of Baptist talk," says one Jesuit. "He can discuss things intelligently, and he's not afraid to argue. He's also a funny guy; we enjoy having him around."

During his stay at Harvard, Glenn tried to go home each weekend to his family in New Jersey. Because his territory covers 16 states, the Iglehearts chose a central location; living in New Jersey also is convenient because New York City, an hour away, is base for several representatives of other denominations and the National Council of Churches. Glenn goes into the city several times a month to meet with such persons, exchanging ideas and information.

> "Well, sure I read the *Book of Mormon.* If I don't, how can I ask a Mormon to look at what we've got?"

Driving home to Jersey on the snow-covered Connecticut turnpike, Glenn talks about some of the things he has learned in his travels and studies.

"People have felt needs that sometimes are not obvious needs," he says.

"Part of the problem is getting through the barrier of apathy by state leaders. It's the old theory of the squeaky wheel getting the oil. Not many people voice a need for a conference on interfaith witness, so there's no call for it."

The cars on the turnpike have slowed to a crawl, their drivers looking nervously at the truck which has jackknifed off the side. The rotating lights of highway patrol cars throw a momentary glare into the night.

Glenn emphasizes his words with his usual energetic hand motions, yet keeps the concentration the slippery road demands.

The windshield wipers slap away half-frozen snow, and he goes on.

"If I were a Baptist in a Catholic community for five years, and there was no 'how to relate to Catholics' conference, I'd be upset."

The key to all interfaith witness is exposure, and that is what Glenn tries to promote. "I used to say 'I'm available,' but now I go with a calendar in hand. I guess I've picked up some aggressiveness."

A major role for Glenn is sharing information, talking to associational directors of missions to get and give ideas.

"A person usually feels more confident if he knows so and so in the next county

did this interfaith witness thing, and he liked it."

When talking to churches or associations, Glenn doesn't force a prepackaged program on them.

"I find out what their needs are, what they want to know about—maybe kids come home from college talking about Bahai or *The Exorcist*—and that's what they want to find out about. Some churches carry out interfaith witness activities Glenn doesn't know about 'til they're over, such as the Baptist-Catholic dialogue held by two Washington, D.C., churches.

Glenn would like to see more such conferences; in the meantime, he's available as a resource for such seminars as the nine on Mormonism held around Washington, D. C., last May.

Since the new Mormon temple opened there, Baptists have been exposed to Mormon beliefs more often.

More than 1,500 Baptists showed up at the conferences to study those beliefs and explore ways of responding to them.

From this group, Glenn got the nucleus of his first interfaith witness associates class, an idea he's been incubating many months. Interfaith witness associates are trained to teach other Baptists about a certain religious faith—in this case what Mormons believe.

The first group of IWAs met last December in Silver Spring, Maryland.

Participants were mailed study materials, then given a pretest when they arrived. Pastors, housewives and student

Glenn's goal is for individual Baptists to feel secure enough to witness to the person next door.

ministers alike scratched their heads as they tried to remember, "Now, let's see, T or F, Mormons believe that single women can go to heaven."

Glenn honored the IWA trainees' time and intelligence. The weekend aimed at four goals: an evaluation of the Mormon beliefs, growth in interpersonal relationships, what the church can do in the area of interfaith witness, and teaching skills to pass along the knowledge.

Friday night the Baptists met two Mormons, Mr. and Mrs. Glenn E. Nielson. Nielson is president of the Washington Mission, which oversees the activity of all Mormon missionaries in the area. They studied the *Book of Mormon* and *Pearl of Great Price*, asked questions and traded ideas. The next day, the trainees looked up references for Mormon beliefs and role-played encounters with Mormons.

They drew interpretative pictures of their ideas of Mormons, planned how to pass along what they'd learned about the Mormon faith to Baptists in their own churches.

As Glenn talks about the guidelines for interfaith witness, he edges up to the table, keeping close eye contact. "Interfaith witness is not judging, not convicting, but sowing seeds," he says. "Witness-

ing is a two-way conversation, a matter of seeing people, not labels.

"Some people say that to read the *Book of Mormon* is to admit there's something in there, for example.

"Well, sure I read the *Book of Mormon*. If I don't, how can I ask a Mormon to look at what we've got?"

When Glenn is talking about another religion, he likes to be sure of his facts. "I don't like for other people to say, 'You read us wrong, we don't believe that.'"

He often asks a person of that faith to appear with him on a panel to "keep me straight," such as the rabbi he invited to a conference on world religions at Averett College in Danville, Virginia.

Glenn stresses that those who study other religious groups need to remain open, seek new information and insight.

T he ideal situation would be—and I have achieved this with some—is where I would be with a group of Baptists and a Jesuit, and the Jesuit can turn and say 'You tell them what we believe.' Because I can accurately represent what a Jesuit does believe."

Glenn points out that what a person thinks about his religion is also tied to his generation and ethnic group.

"You can't talk about 'Catholics,'" he says, "You have to ask, 'Which Catholics? What part of the country?'"

As an example, he mentions that six Catholic girls attend the Bible study in his home in New Jersey, and they represent the wide range of today's Catholics.

"Some have not been touched by the things that are happening in the Catholic church, bad or good," Glenn says. "Some are upset; they don't believe in the ritual anymore; some are just asking questions.

"You can't pigeonhole all the Catholics,

just as all Baptists aren't alike."

Not pigeonholing persons of a religious group means more discretion in choosing a Baptist to speak or witness to them.

"If a Catholic is older, more authoritarian, looks up to the priest, then I would ask a pastor to speak," Glenn says. "If a Catholic is turned off by his church, then a pastor might be the worst one to meet with him."

Each religion has its idiosyncrasies, and Glenn tries to explain those as well.

"One thing I learned at Harvard, for instance, was to make some of the distinctions in language. Like "Quran" instead of "Koran," because that's how Muslims prefer it.

"I'd like to help people realize that you never call somebody a Mohammedan — Muslim is the correct term. This can help prevent misunderstanding and ill will from the start."

Interpreting the silent language and gestures of different faiths is a subject in itself.

Even certain colors have significance. Glenn recalls that at one Baptist-Jewish banquet, the visitors, older Jewish women, cooled visibly when they saw the yellow table decorations.

Glenn explains that yellow was the color armbands Nazis made the Jews wear during World War II. "It still has a bad connotation for them."

Glenn has collected art, pictures and calligraphy symbolizing each religion's faith. He believes that much can be shown through religious art — the 38 signs of Buddha, for instance.

In Hinduism, religious figures show lots of arms and legs. "I used to think that was just a lot of confusion, but after I studied it, I found out that to the Hindu, the more arms and legs it has, the more power it signifies. And where they are is important."

At the Baptist-Muslim dialogue in Toledo last spring, Glenn knew the terms, the concepts. "I may not have always pronounced them right," he laughs, "but some imams [leader of a mosque] were a little amazed. My whole three months at Harvard helped me prepare for those three days."

Doing his homework shows the position from which Glenn always approaches persons of other religions — a position of respect.

"We shouldn't just say, 'Here, you need this,'" he says. "There's a difference, starting where God wants us to start, then offering out of what store we have to meet a person's need."

After one Baptist-Catholic dialogue, Glenn was reporting the event to a Baptist group. After he finished, one Baptist man walked up and, looking somewhat puzzled, said, "We sent you up there to win them, not to join them."

Glenn not only hasn't joined "them," he remains convinced that understanding other faith's beliefs can help Baptists be stronger Baptists and more active members of a Christian community. •

Baptists believe they have "the answer." But they share the world with millions of others who are equally sure they have the answer.

SMITH

In Watts, some problems need a scalpel instead of a bandage. Arnette and Sid Smith help churches reach out to heal the hurts.

Sid Smith and two other black students had just gotten settled in their motel room. It was 1963, and they were attending the Texas Baptist Student Union meeting in Abilene. Then came a knock on the door. Their BSU director came in and said, "Uh, I'd like to talk to you."

They asked what was up; he nervously answered that the manager had told him black students would have to eat in the ballroom instead of the restaurant.

"Let's all leave," Sid replied. "I don't want any part of a place like this."

A bit later the BSU director returned, "Okay, you can eat in the restaurant."

Sid later found out he had rounded up the other directors and gone to the motel manager. "We're pulling out—all 600 people—if the blacks can't eat with us." The manager had conceded.

"I have had some supportive experiences like that with whites," says Sid, who grew up in central Texas. "But, in the whole area of race relations in the SBC, we still have a long way to go. A long way."

Arnette, a teacher who just finished her master's, instills healthy attitudes toward racial matters at both school and church.

Sid can recount other stories. Some he tells with a certain amount of astonished glee, a "here's one you'll appreciate" attitude.

The years have dulled the painfulness of such experiences, and perhaps it is easier to laugh now. Yet a certain amount of bitterness remains, and a definite desire for change.

It is partly that feeling which fuels Sid's desire to improve race relations, especially through Christian social ministries. While studying for his doctorate, he wrote his thesis on the interracial church, studying 20 examples in California.

The big missionary says with a slow smile, "I learned that the concept of the integrated church is not with us very well. My conviction is that in a multiethnic community, the only kind of goal that is healthy is a multiethnic group."

You couldn't pick a more "multiethnic" metropolis than Los Angeles. About 17 percent of L.A. is black—that's nearly 700,000 people. One million Chicanos live here, plus thousands of Orientals and other ethnic groups. In Compton, where Sid is based, 80 percent of the 80,000 residents are black. High taxes and high crime are common complaints. Schools have their share of problems, too.

Sid's wife, Arnette, who teaches third grade, says, "Just because you have a black principal and black staff in a predominantly black school doesn't mean you're going to solve all the problems."

Today Sid and Arnette are missionaries in Watts, a part of Los Angeles whose name would still be unfamiliar to most Americans if not for its racial troubles 10 years ago. In his own way, Sid is encouraging the churches of his association to move more forcefully into their communities.

Sid and Arnette live in Carson, about 15 miles from downtown L.A. Sid's office is in the pink stucco building of First Baptist Church, Compton, a racially mixed congregation. From there he drives his green VW to Baptist churches all over south central L.A.

Just getting in the VW is time-consuming, for Sid stands 6'4" and weighs 250. Even with the small car, Sid's monthly gas bill runs more than $100, for the suburbs of south central L.A. are miles apart.

Someone once called Los Angeles "40 suburbs in search of a city." That was after World War II, and the suburbs are still looking for identity.

California has a cadence all its own, and L.A.'s personality nearly defies definition. The name of Watts, for instance, brings to mind the riots of 1965. But the area doesn't fit the stereotype of an eastern inner city.

Watts sprawls over several hundred blocks. Small houses, frame or stucco, line the residential streets. Several have been repossessed and boarded up, a few abandoned cars and shells of small business buildings dot the neighborhoods. On the surface, the atmosphere seems mild, unthreatening—just vaguely blah.

Outsiders likely would look at Watts and ask, "Riots—here?"

For one thing, the sun shines. Through the smog, true, but it shines. Mean annual temperature is 64 degrees; you can expect

15 inches of rain a year. And the signs of poverty, frustration and unfulfilled dreams are not as visible as in an older city's pallid complexion of crowded apartment buildings and dirty tenements.

Yet the surface signs cannot mask the still-healing wounds of Watts eruptions 10 years ago. And it is in this environment that Sid tries to foster cooperative Christian ministries between blacks and whites.

The task is overwhelming. It's a temptation to apply a Band-Aid when you need to demand a scalpel.

But Sid has made a try. For starters, he organized a ministry for prisoners, CRASH, that grew out of concerns developed in his days as a prison guard at San Quentin in San Francisco.

While attending Golden Gate seminary, Sid had been making $1.40 an hour planting house plants. One morning he saw a friend in a guard's uniform leaving for work.

"Hey, man, where you going?" Sid asked.

"When he said San Quentin, I asked him if they were hiring," Sid recalls. "I went over and took the test and there I was."

He worked as a San Quentin guard for three years. "It was just a job for money at first, then it turned out to be much more."

Sid saw firsthand how prison changes a man. "Once you go through the big gate, it's monotonous. Same clothes as everybody else, eat at the same time, go to bed at the same time."

Sid saw nearly every kind of crime inside the prison that is committed outside: theft, homosexual rape, even murder.

He's thought about writing a book on his experiences. "I'd call it *The Diary of a San Quentin Bull.* There's plenty to write about. I know what it means to be a bull — a mature bull."

Prison changes not only inmates, but guards as well. Sid still bears scars from a scalding incident, and was hit with honey buckets several times. "I had to redefine myself," he says. "You learn to psyche yourself up. If a convict attacks, you already know what to do.

"You have to reach a balance. I got to the point where I could say, 'I may teach you a religion course in the morning and talk about love, but in the afternoon, I am Officer Smith, and if you try to escape, I will have to shoot you.'"

Sid taught the religion course through a black prisoners' organization, SATE (Self-Advancement Through Education). Later the men asked him to become their sponsor.

Through his experiences at San Quentin, Sid realized how badly constructive prison reform was needed. And these thoughts later evolved into the program called CRASH.

CRASH stands for Christians Responding and Serving Humanity. It helps educate people about prison reform and finds ways each volunteer can contribute — through a person-to-person match with an inmate or job-hunting for released prisoners, for instance.

The program began about three years ago after Sid preached a sermon at

Sid likes being a Christian social minister. "You have more freedom. I'm limited only by my ability to get people involved."

Greenleaf Baptist Church in Whittier.

He emphasized two things:

First, the criminal justice system has failed — here's how. And second, I feel I have a responsibility as a Christian to be a redemptive force in this area.

After this sermon, 13 people responded, and CRASH was born. Sid estimates 250 church members have volunteered to work with prisoners since that time. About 40 are active now.

In Sid's bookcase, *Attica* is shelved next to *Mission to America,* Arthur Rutledge's book about home missions. That accidental placement reveals a little about Sid's combination of Christianity and social concern.

"We need to emphasize a *healthy* system of corrections," Sid says. He feels Christians should learn about the needs for correctional systems, then change those systems, both through institutional structures and as individuals.

How does an individual get involved in CRASH? Richard Redding, an X-ray technician from Florida, and his wife, Judy, heard Sid speak at Village Baptist Church in Downey. They volunteered, then Sid visited them. "Our choir sang for prisoners at the youth training center," says Judy, a former medical transcriber. "I didn't really think they'd care," she tells Sid. "They didn't act like it at first. But since then we've gotten letters from them. That may seem like a

"Urban man doesn't have to go to the mountains to find God."

trivial thing, but . . . ."

Sid shakes his head, no. It may seem like a small thing, but it is a first step.

As Judy bounces her son Nathan on her lap, Sid explains some options.

• writing and visiting man to man, woman to woman. An individual is matched to an inmate—to write, visit, sometimes to find jobs after release.

• helping people on parole—"One real need is for friends—and not the same friends they had before."

• working in a parole group home—"If you have a skill, you could teach it in the

group home—sewing or typing, for instance."

• researching the prison structures and supporting legislation on prison reform.

"I'd like to get right down to it," Judy declares. "Where do we start?"

Sid recommends the California Institute for Women and California Institute for Men. "You'll need to write, then go establish a relationship," he explains. "But I will make the first contact.

"We do have some openings—I know some chaplains," he says. A go-between such as Sid is necessary.

If an individual just wrote a letter to a prison, it likely would go to the director of activities. "He'd scratch his head and say, 'Well, I never heard of these folks.' He'd ask you to fill out an information sheet and refer it to a committee," Sid says. "They're skeptical, especially of religious groups."

One of the most visible outgrowths of CRASH was the House of Agape, a parole group home that opened in May, 1971. The small, one-story building on Wilmington Street sheltered 35 teenagers in three years.

Sid started from scratch. He needed a place, furnishings, people to run it, a system to get the young people to live there, and $1,800 for the first month's operating expenses. "One by one, our needs were met," Sid says. "Two people gave us buildings. I got a guy I knew in San Quentin to run it for six weeks. We got the churches to furnish one apartment each."

The chaplain at the California Institute for Women recommended his secretary to be the resident counselor. She and her husband had been in prison for narcotics possession. She got an early parole, because of this new job.

Two parole agents committed themselves to assign young people to the halfway house.

The House of Agape had mixed effectiveness. For instance, Sid had a 100 percent success rate in finding jobs for the parolees, but not nearly so high an average in getting them to keep the jobs.

Only two people ran away, and that's a good rate for a group home. But the house was hit by vandals again and again.

The house contracted with the California Youth Authority, the juvenile criminal justice division in the state, to take care of the parolees. Later the state switched its contract, and the House of Agape had trouble getting funds.

The combination of vandalism and lack of money caused the house to close three years after it opened.

But Sid says, "I think it was good for Christians to have their name associated with that sort of thing. It was good for Southern Baptists. It gave them a good image in interracial matters."

The House of Agape helped bring the association's Baptists together around a project, although Sid admits some people were uneasy about it.

"They are the ones who have the image of the soul brother with the razor in his pocket, wearing a dashiki and a Super Fly hat. But that's ridiculous.

"Most of the white church members reacted quite well."

CRASH volunteers sometimes found unusual settings for their ministries. Dave Thompson, a religion student at USC, began a karate class at a Watts parole center.

Brian Sun, a black belt from Taiwan, visited Dave's class once to give a test, but stayed and got involved too. He now teaches the boys.

The class in *taekwondo,* a Korean martial art similar to karate, meets three times a week. The room is filled with black youngsters, most wearing baggy white trousers and shirts.

Fists flail and pop as Brian exhorts his students to practice a triple punch. "Ready, punch, kick!" Brian yells. "Don't pitty-pat, Curtis, don't pitty-pat!"

As the boys jump and spin and kick, Brian points out ones who have won trophies at meets. Mastering the skills gives them a sense of power, accomplishment, pride. And, Sid hopes, a healthy self-image helps steer young people away from further crime.

California averages $11,000 to keep a person in prison, but about one fourth that to keep him out on supervision.

"It's usually in that first 90 days when they decide whether to stay out of prison.

"I would like to see a church in each of our communities be the first one to greet a person when he gets out," Sid says.

The concept of a church ministering

with its community also led to the twin-triplet program.

In 1965, while Watts was still burning after massive riots and looting, Jack O'Neal, California director of cooperative ministries with National Baptists, called E.V. Hill, a prominent National Baptist pastor in Watts. "Ed, I'm watching all this on TV," he said, "What can we as Southern Baptists do?"

One thing they tried was saturating the area with the gospel—and they started through Vacation Bible Schools.

Hill's church, Mt. Zion, sponsored four VBSes the next summer; the Home Mission Board sent four summer missionaries to help.

In 1967, Mt. Zion sponsored 10 VBSes and the Board sent more student missionaries.

In 1968, Mt. Zion had a goal of 100. They didn't quite make that, but they did have 82, reaching 6,000 people.

Out of this flurry of activity came the idea for the twin-triplet program. Sid came to L.A. in September, 1968. He wanted to extend VBSes into backyards, garages, wherever he and the churches could find a spot to meet.

In 1969, five area churches had 10 VBSes each. In 1970, the element of twin-

continued on page 152

Sid and Arnette belong to a church that knows from experience how to adapt to an interracial situation.

To encourage Christians to minister
with their communities, Sid promotes
Rent-a-Teen and CRASH. The teen program
creates awareness and pride in working.
CRASH gives church members an outlet
to work with prisoners and support a
constructive system of criminal justice.

Fists flail and pop as Brian Sun instructs
a karate class at a Watts parole center.
Under Sid's leadership, CRASH volunteers
sometimes find unusual settings,
such as this one, for their ministries.

The twin/triplet program teams black, white and Spanish churches to plan VBSes in backyards, garages, wherever. Each team holds at least 10 schools.

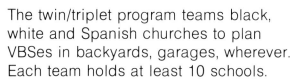

Operation Get Together, an outgrowth
of twin/triplet VBS, brings churches
together to eat, talk, pray and share.
Sid keeps busy—a TV talk show
on prison reform one day,
substitute preaching the next.

Taped worship services give shut-ins an opportunity to be part of the church. Sid tried to start a broader ministry to older persons, and Toland and Dolores Lewis helped. But that project is still in the birthing stage.

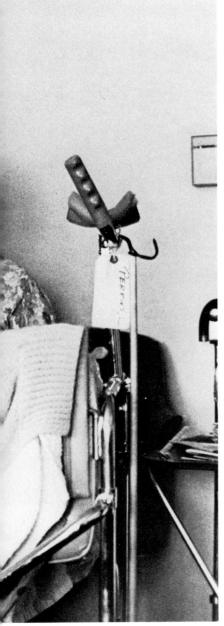

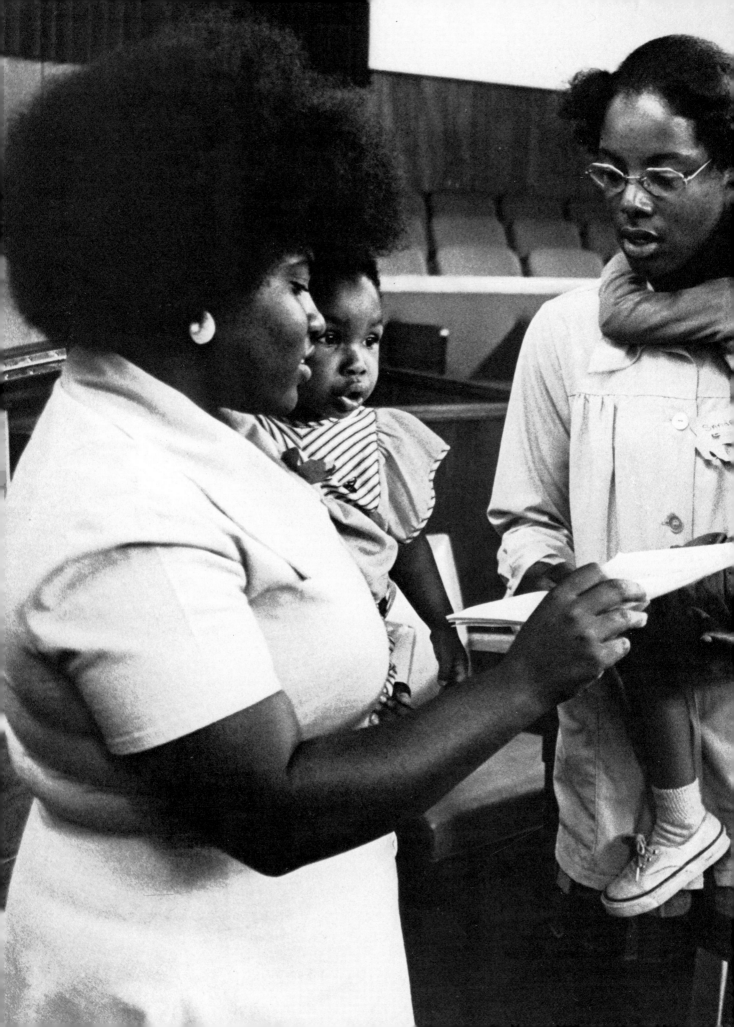

Student summer missionaries come to L.A.
to help with VBS and other interracial
projects. Last summer's group made and wore
matching dashikis, and that's a symbol
of their closeness and camaraderie.
One of Sid's great delights is watching
the students grow, change, contribute.

ning was added, pairing three white churches with three black churches. In 1971, Sid expanded that to the triplet program, bringing in Spanish churches.

In 1974, a dozen churches, including a Chinese church, cooperated in triplet or twin programs. Each team of churches has to hold at least 10 VBSes. "Many have never held more than one VBS," Sid says. "At first, they say—'Naw, 10? We can't do 10.' But they do."

Since the twin-triplet program began, 12,000 have attended VBS, and 900 professions of faith have been made.

You can get a glimpse of the twin program in action by looking at First Baptist of Compton, pastored by Willie Simmons, and a white church in Lynwood, pastored by Herb Carson.

Several years ago Compton began changing from all-white to black. So did Compton church, experiencing the same transitional pains.

The 30-year-old church once had 800 for services, now they average fewer than 100. But the congregation is making a slow upturn; the membership is now about 50 percent white, 50 percent black.

"We've been having race relations Sunday for 10 years now," says Simmons.

"I'd like to see us come to the point where we don't even have to have it, where we have just learned to work together as people of God. The opportunity to know each other will be a big benefit of the triplet program.

"When I asked our people if they wanted to cooperate in the triplet program, one man said, 'How can we afford not to?'" Simmons recalls.

Sid says because of the triplet-twin program, several churches have redefined themselves, developing an appreciation of other cultures.

And Simmons sees other long-range results. "I hope we'll be able to serve as a resource for places like the Sunday School Board. I hope we'll have some answers for them on how to minister better to Spanish-speaking, blacks, Chicanos.

"When we bring in the literature, and you have 100 black kids but no black faces in the books, they say, 'Man, I can't identify with this. They say God cares for every-body, but there are no black faces.'"

The twin program also works well in a suburb farther out, like Fontana, a community of 20,000 about 45 miles northeast of Compton. Sid used to jog with J. Edward Henry, pastor of the First Baptist Church of Fontana, a black congregation.

The two friends talked about setting up a twin program in Fontana, and Henry called Elton Turner, a white neighboring pastor at Tamerind Avenue Baptist Church. Together they invited Sid to talk.

"That threw me off course a little," laughs Turner. "Sid didn't look like any missionary I'd ever met."

Turner's church became enthusiastic about the concept. "By June of '72, we got it going. At the end of summer, we committed ourselves to do it again, if we could be partners with First Baptist Church."

All summer long, you could find a VBS somewhere in Fontana. Evening VBSes were common; those in backyards, garages and parks were, too.

Sid asked if the twins could find a place to put a summer missionary to work. They could, and did.

Elton Turner says his church followed up on those who made decisions during VBS. "Our church has its major ministry with kids up to about junior high age, so our church is especially receptive to these ministries like this.

"The fact that we have the interest to obligate ourselves to this kind of program says something of our attitude—a basic love of the Lord we have always shared in common.

"This church has had very open pastors throughout the years," says Turner, "so I can't take credit for people's attitudes."

Henry says one of the big changes he has noticed has been "in our relationships—we respond all during the year, not just summer."

The churches have had joint services and attended each other's revivals.

Henry and Turner have exchanged pulpits, such as on race relations Sunday.

"The other night we shared a potluck dinner," Henry goes on, "and I was saying how glad I was now, when we're having fellowship, we don't have to say, 'We're going over to see the white folks.' It's just friends."

Turner says, "If the churches who are talking about their problems would just pay us a visit—we feel that confident in

Sid believes in confronting people with what they're capable of becoming. "It's a Christian's responsibility."

our relationship—they would see what we're talking about, the way our relationship has grown."

Another set of twins is in La Puente, where Norris Fulfer is pastor at First Baptist, a white church. E.W. McCall is pastor at St. Stephen Baptist Church, a National Baptist church.

"Fulfer and I were always close," McCall says. "But our churches hadn't found it. The twin program has broken the barrier, caused awareness. We found out we have mutual problems and mutual solutions."

"I don't know that there have been any great crisis situations," says Fulfer. "It's just a matter of time and relationships, coming to know one another."

They have been in the twin program three years. "It's very successful," Fulfer says, "especially the backyard VBS. Catholic, Methodist, it doesn't matter—everybody comes. The only problem is getting enough adults to be involved."

Ninety percent of Fulfer's neighborhood is Catholic; several Catholic parents have helped with VBS, especially in bringing refreshments.

Not much publicity is needed. "We just tack up a sign, 'VBS will be here from 6:00-8:00' or whatever. The kids just come," Fulfer says. A VBS in Fulfer's backyard drew 25, then 55, then 60—"that was the most the yard would hold," he smiles.

Teachers structure VBS lessons to meet the needs of each group.

"The teenagers have really enjoyed Bible study," Fulfer says. "They studied questions like, 'What do you do with anger when you are so mad at your parents you could kill them. How does the Bible answer this?' The youth chose the topics, then got in on their own problems."

"The twin program helped take our church into the community," says McCall.

"We only have two or three families within walking distance of our church, the rest are spread out. So finally our church reached out to where they were living, through the backyard VBS."

In La Puente, the twin VBS program has expanded to a year-round cooperation —as Operation Get Together. The two churches have a "prayer and share" pro-gram, getting together at least once a month to talk, pray, eat and share.

Although St. Stephen's church is predominantly white, about 30 Spanish-speaking people attend. Fulfer once asked his congregation how many of them had eaten in a black or Spanish home, and admits to being surprised when about half the people raised their hands.

"One of the best ways to get to know each other," McCall says, "is breaking bread together. There's something about eating together, you're able to communicate. It's easier to spring from a cup of coffee to something else."

To help with the VBSes and other programs, the HMB sends summer missionaries. Sid is their supervisor. To work in the racially mixed setting, Sid gets a mixed group of students. Last summer, for instance, two white girls, two black girls, two white boys and one Hawaiian boy served.

And one of Sid's great delights is watch-

ing them change through the 10 weeks.

The students are affected not only by the California culture and Watts environment, but by Sid himself.

At the end of last summer, student Russ Jeeter, a white from Louisiana, recalled, "My first impression of Sid was oh, my gosh, I'm going to have to work with *him* all summer?"

On first glance, Sid may come across with the flashy flamboyance of a Reverend Ike. He favors black patent shoes and patterned socks, drives a gold Monte Carlo as his family car.

"Some probably consider me a radical," Sid says, then laughs. "I don't."

But another side of Sid can show him subdued, straight, black suit-white shirt, depending on the occasion and the company.

The summer missionaries see both sides, many sides, through their weekly group meetings with Sid. The meetings may be on the ride out to Disneyland or Paramount studios, for Sid loves to combine work and play. He both talks and listens, periodically—almost habitually— reassuring the students, "I hear you, I hear you." But the camaraderie helps develop a closeness that contributes to the ministries in an interracial situation.

Not all church members in south central L.A. are open to the idea of ministries such as CRASH and interracial VBS, however. "They lack a Christian concept of social action or don't have the time, and many probably are not ready for the idea of a minority leader," Sid believes.

Other members itch about numbers— how many were saved through this ministry, how many decisions? When Sid can scratch with numbers, they don't complain.

Sid's programs have been allies to the association, not strangers. One result is the association mission action committee, which was set up last fall. It will lead the association in education, training and direct leadership.

To further move the church into the community, Sid has helped with Rent-a-Teen program, cooperating with American

Baptists. Ivan George, Sid's American Baptist counterpart, directs the program.

Rent-a-Teen finds part-time odd jobs and matches them to teenagers. Jobs like painting, carpet cleaning and yard work help instill a skill and pride in working.

Two summers ago, a selected group of five boys and two girls went out to outlying counties to wash windows, clean lots and other odd jobs. They lived there a week in homes, the youth center, or a church basement.

"They get to meet different people," George says, "and, for a while anyway, be in a different environment. Also the people in the communities get a better understanding of the youngsters.

"When those people thought of youngsters from the inner city they thought of project housing, no clothes, poor manners. But they found out different."

In all, about 80 teenagers were involved last summer. To get more jobs next summer, George and Sid plan to increase the publicity, begin it sooner and line up better liaisons in each church. Because they know that in many projects, results haven't matched expectations.

Sid and the people he works with have had their share of disappointments, failures, frustrations.

Doris Dugmore recalls trying to start an interracial group for singles. "We had bowling and parties, but it didn't work," she says.

"For instance at one party we ended up with all black men and all white women. They did not feel comfortable. The lady having the party was scared and didn't want to have any more parties in her home."

Because of such feelings, and because of lack of interest, the program eventually died out.

"That was a significant example to me." Sid says. "because it pointed out we may not be able to pick up examples from a monoracial situation and use them successfully in a multiracial situation.

"On the other hand," he backtracks, "what is our alternative? One temptation is to say, 'Let's have two groups, one black and one white.' The other is to realize that there are some things we *can't* do without compromising our Christian morals. We just have to let the idea die—'til people are ready for an interracial group."

Patience doesn't always come easy for

Sid, though. He has some strong, often-voiced words on Southern Baptists' attitudes in race relations, and on the direction churches and the convention as a whole should take.

"As a convention, the SBC hasn't seen anything yet in terms of the race problem," Sid believes. "The stage is gradually being set for the Southern Baptist activist. There are not many now, but dissatisfaction is growing.

"The headaches we've had before, such as the student protest at Denver, will come back again, in different forms.

"Some awareness will come from getting in and having some painful experiences — being brutally honest," Sid says. "Then staying in there and building back up from a position of honesty.

We need to kill the concept of ministering by proxy. There is a certain hypocrisy. We need to learn to build a fellowship so that we care about each other, so that there will be no such thing as a black brother or white brother, but that just happens to be the color of his skin."

If the SBC has not turned full circle, in Sid's opinion, then why does he stay?

"Well, other denominations have their problems too.

"If you switched, you'd have to start all over again in the structure. You have to work yourself up in any group and that takes time. In some denominations you can't be a general 'til you're an old man. Here, I had an opportunity. I might not get it somewhere else."

Since a minority doesn't have the power of numbers, what powers does it have?

"You can focus public opinion on the problem," Sid says. "Put on an educational campaign to sensitize people."

As a last resort, he thinks disruptions sometimes work. "After all the smoke clears away, you can get down to a discussion of the issues.

"You can create new structures to meet the needs. Organizational efforts work sometimes — nominating people even when you know they can't be elected — to create awareness."

Sid stored away his rose-colored glasses long ago, but retains a semi-militant, semi-optimistic attitude.

If the changes in the past 10 years are any indication, and Sid believes they are, these hopes are justified.

When Sid was in University of Corpus Christi a decade ago, for instance, he was once asked his opinion on the racial situation.

"I said, 'Problems? I don't see any problems.' Because at that time I was defining 'no problems' as the absence of tension.

"My senior year was the first time I was really aware of anything, I think," he remembers. "There was a white girl in one of my classes. I was a little scared, you know, it was like forbidden fruit, but she was the sort of girl I liked, so one day, I asked her for a Coke in the student union."

Walking back, Sid ran into his boss, the superintendent of maintenance, a white man in his 40s. "He gave me the old dog-eye, you know. And later on he took me aside and threatened to fire me the next time he saw me with a white girl."

Sid, the student, was bothered by this

One involved pastor says, "I'm so glad that now, when we're having fellowship, we don't have to say, 'We're going over to see the white folks.' It's just friends."

at first, but says in a way "it was sort of liberating. I learned I could be right and be persecuted. That was a very important lesson for me to learn. From then on, I was psychologically free."

He has built on that freedom, and the changes in society, to propel himself to a position of responsibility and some power.

Ultimately, Sid's ministries in Watts and south central L.A. may boil down to this: The success story is not in the activities themselves, but in what else might be happening if no Christian social ministers were there at all. •

TREMAINE

He is preacher, father, athlete, counselor. And the protean missionary adapts easily into situations in New Mexico, Florida, Massachusetts.

"This kid overdosed one time and we went up there and he was blue," says Bob Tremaine, frowning with the memory. "His brother was there when it happened, but his brother was also a drug user. He knew his brother had bought from a new guy and when he OD'ed on the amount he normally used, he knew the new guy was selling some pretty good junk."

Instead of taking care of his brother, he ran to find the seller of this purer drug. Bob shakes his head sadly.

"Another night a guy was staggering down the street. I'd met him a few days before, found out where he lived. I took him home and began trying to love that guy." It was a long haul, Bob says, but now the man is directing a Christian alcoholic rehabilitation center.

Drunks, kids on drugs, teenagers with nowhere to go: Bob Tremaine talked and listened to them all. In seven years in the inner city of Worcester, Massachusetts, Bob saw so much of the first kind of situation that it angered and hardened him. He

saw enough of the second to reassure him that his ministry there was valid.

Both situations were far different from the middle class church Bob pastored in Hobbs, New Mexico. In the years in Worcester, before he moved to Florida last fall, such situations changed and challenged him.

Worcester, the second largest city in Massachusetts, is built on seven hills. In the inner city, narrow, winding streets are lined with crowded walk-up apartments, high-rises and shells of burned out buildings. Hundreds of old people—many of them alone and lonely—pass their days here. So do thousands of teenagers.

Worcester's skyline is dotted with church steeples, yet many of its people are untouched by Christian concern. In the '60s, the area was selected as a Model Cities project because of its poor housing, social and economic conditions. It was an inner city with all an inner city's complex problems.

Into that situation came Bob and Glenda Tremaine and their children, Tim and Tori (Tara was born four years later).

In New Mexico, Bob had led a church that was "nearly dead" to become the fastest growing church, in both attendance and giving, in the state. "But we had felt a call to missions," says Glenda, a warm, open woman who met Bob in school at Hardin-Simmons.

Bob was New Mexico's representative to the Home Mission Board for two years, and spent much extra time doing projects. In 1967, the Tremaines were appointed by the Home Mission Board to work in Worcester, about 35 miles from Boston.

The Board had bought an 80-year-old Congregational church building in the inner city, and wanted to use the large, red-stone building to start mission work.

"There was a Bible study that had come out of some revival services in '65 or so. This Bible study had about 13 people in it and that's what we came to when we came to Worcester," Bob says. The jobs of pastor and director of Baptist ministries are challenging under any circumstances, but especially in a new culture. Yet Bob had the credentials and the self-confidence to tackle them.

Tremaine's very size is imposing— 6'6", 260 pounds—and, some would say, with an ego to match it. A handsome, former All-American basketball player, he exudes an obvious, outward self-confidence. Well-read, personable, a good speaker . . . the adjectives roll on. If Bob Tremaine did have a solid self-image, it was understandable.

"He comes on strong," says a friend, "but he has done things up there nobody else would think of doing."

If Bob had waited for Worcester to come to typical activities in the red-bricked building, nothing much might have happened. Instead he reached out to Worcester. Bob started by meeting the people where they were—on the street. It was an eye-opening new culture.

"I'd go out on the street at 9:00 at night until 2:00 in the morning. I'd sit on the little ledge in front of the church and just talk to people. You walk around and you always find somebody who needs help."

Help could be as little as whipping kids around a snow-packed parking lot from a rope on the back of Bob's VW.

Aiming for longer term, more substantial help for kids with no place to go, he opened the church basement as a coffeehouse. Summer missionaries sifted through the junk in the cellar, constructed some partitions, hustled some wooden spools for tables.

The cellar wasn't heated at the time; it was so cold you could see your breath. But the people came, for coffee, conversation and Bible study.

Bob felt the church building should be used as many hours as possible. At first, the coffeehouse, "Lost and Found," was open three nights a week. Later it shifted to Friday nights only. Attendance fluctuated—a couple of dozen one night, more than 200 on others.

"Sometimes it was just crammed," Bob says. "But that's not really good. If you can keep the noise level down where it's just a quiet sort of togetherness, people are more open to talk."

And many of the people who came did have problems to talk about. "We believe in listening first and then sharing," says the missionary. "Kids would come in and wouldn't get hassled in there.

With Glenda, his wife, Bob has ministered as a pastor, inner city missionary and church starter in a planned community.

"We had kids who would come to the coffeehouse, they had shot up with heroin or something, and they'd be just as spaced out as they could be.

"This just kept happening. After folks just consistently nodded out, and you don't know what to do with them, you get the message that something is going on.

"That's when we started looking for some help," Bob goes on. "There wasn't any. Then some Jaycees arranged for some training which we didn't take long to find out was inadequate. It was professional people talking to us about a professional way of looking at it, and that just wasn't where the street thing was."

Not that a pastor from New Mexico had all the answers either.

From the "Lost and Found" — and the human needs Bob and Glenda observed — grew a weekend project, the crisis center and hot line. It eventually developed into a full-blown community ministry.

"We just used our church," Bob says. "If anyone was head of the crisis center, I was. Just developed the training for it. Which at first wasn't very good, because nobody knew anything."

Church members and students from nearby colleges volunteered to staff the center. The crisis center put out its shingle — hot line open 6:00 on Friday until 11:00 Sunday — but even before opening day, the phone started ringing.

"We got all kinds of calls," Bob says, "suicides, elderly people who were just lonely. And they didn't wait 'til 6:00 on Friday to call. We got a call from this father and he said his son was gonna commit suicide. When we got there, the rope was over the tree limb, the chair was there and he was putting the rope around his neck. I just slowly, very slowly, walked over and said how are you doing. We got him calmed down.

"We had to answer another suicide thing and the guy stuck a gun out at us.

"I'd learned from experience when we knocked, always to stand to the side. When he came out and did that, I just kicked the door and knocked it off the hinges. I took the gun away from him.

"We stayed with him. We got him in a veterans' hospital on three occasions.

"He's now a member of one of our missions. So that's one you like to tell about."

It quickly became apparent that for the crisis center, weekend hours just wouldn't get it. Soon the crisis center was open every night, and within six months, 24 hours a day.

The center spawned other ministries. One room in the cellar was the home of the buddy, bucket and blanket club.

"We had kids in there who would try to stop using heroin, and they'd be going cold turkey. We'd give them a blanket to keep warm and a bucket to throw up in and a buddy to sit with them."

About 50 teenagers went through the BB&B club. Some it helped, some it didn't. "I learned weird things from the bad trip room," Bob says. "One winter I came in and I had on a pair of gun gloves, mittens made so your trigger finger is free.

"This girl was in there and they just weren't able to hold her down.

"My nose was cold and I reached up with my glove still on and rubbed it. When she saw the finger move away from what she thought was the mitten, she really flipped. Because she was halucinating anyhow."

Bob took his glove off and the girl squeezed his hand, screamed and cried.

"She and I developed a pretty good relationship because she thought she had done something for me . . . saved my hand from disintegrating."

There may be better ways of helping drug users, but when no help was available, "we just did with what we had,"

Despite his bulk, Tremaine isn't loud-spoken or bombastic.

Bob says. He spent some time in Yale's Drug Dependency Institute and developed teacher training in different school systems.

"This opened doors for me into different communities," he says. And, to symbolize recognition of his work in that area, Worcester officials gave Bob the key to the city.

The church sponsored the crisis center more than two years. "The biggest part of my time was that way," Bob recalls. "I had come to the place where it had to be full-time crisis center or full-time church, one or the other."

So the church went looking for paid staff. Several things worked out so they succeeded. "We got the first floor at the city hospital out-patient building for free. They incorporated our crisis center into a larger program. The drug center is there."

In seeing the fear and frustration caused by conditions in the inner city, Bob's attitudes changed. He moved from a stance of "super-sympathetic" to "almost hostility."

"You see all the poverty and grief and you get sort of overwhelmed by it," he says, "feeling sorry for everybody.

"Then, after we'd been ripped off so many times at the church—the crisis center was broken into, at one point, 23 times in 14 months—we finally had to put somebody in the building 24 hours a day. We put in steel-plated doors and heavy wire screens."

Bob's face turns stern.

"An elderly person's in danger walking one block from the high-rise up Main Street. You see a little old lady who has to pin her house key to her slip strap and carry her coin purse in her hand because she knows if she doesn't, she'll lose her purse.

You go next door in the cellar and find 40 purses chucked in the corner and you see people do it and you stop them and they say, no, we didn't.

"When they leave people to die on the doorsteps of your church . . . when we had the crisis center, they'd just drop them and ring the bell and run."

His forehead wrinkled with the memory, he stops for breath.

"You'd see the police make a bust and run up the stairs. Every junkie on the street would follow and stand on the ground by the building."

They knew as soon as the police knocked on the door, all the drugs in the apartment would either go down the commode or out the window. "And they are praying for manna from heaven," Bob says.

After being sympathetic at first, then going to the other end of being downright angry, Bob came to "an in-between place."

"I don't really trust anyone 'til they've proven themselves now," he says. "I have hundreds of illustrations of those coming in saying, 'It's an emergency, I gotta get to South Carolina, my father's dying,' stuff you really have to check.

"If somebody is really serious and wants help, I'll do everything I can to support him."

He mentions Madeline, a woman in her 60s who came to church one Sunday morning and wanted money to eat.

"I told her I didn't have any, but I said, if you are hungry, come back at 12:15 and I'll see you get something to eat. She did, and we dealt with her. We said come back the next day and she did.

"She's still gaming a bit. She said she needed $5 for a deposit and it was really $2. But she is making some progress. I still go along with that because she has made a commitment to herself to improve her condition.

"But if somebody's just there for a rip-off, like they do—they work every church—I don't have time for that." Yet Bob tries never to shut the door to the extent that a person won't come back.

"I always try. We had some homosexuals who were trying to turn people on in the coffeehouse and it came to the point where they wouldn't be real with us. So

At first, Bob tried to wrap his arms around the whole city of Worcester, starting nearly more ministries than one man could handle.

I said, 'Anytime you want help, I'm the first guy to come to because I'll do all I can. But as long as you're gonna game and try to hurt other people, we just can't have it.'"

As Bob and Glenda worked with the people in the community, they also helped church members expand their concept of "church."

"I believe a church has to get outside the building and stop referring to the building as the church," Bob says firmly. "We had parking lot concerts and rallies in front of city hall, things like this.

"One time the police busted 27 Puerto Ricans for selling dope, and the next day they were all back on the streets on bail. They killed the two guys they thought had framed them.

"We were trying to have a Spanish service on Main Street in front of the church, but we couldn't get anybody to come because the Puerto Rican community was uptight.

"On Saturday we went down to where they killed the two guys on Friday and that's where we had our service. We drew a crowd."

And the crowd drew the police, who thought they had a riot on their hands until somebody reported, "No, it's just pastor Tremaine, holding a service."

That wasn't his only brush with danger in the street.

"A guy tried to use a knife on me one night. He and three of his buddies threatened to kill me if I wouldn't take this guy to his wife—they were divorced and he couldn't find her. He put a knife to my throat and said he'd kill me if I didn't do what he wanted me to do."

The large, thick fingers spread wide and it seems hard to imagine the big man not having the upper hand. But Bob says that's not the point.

"I learned some real spiritual things there. You're either going to do it in his power, or your power, and if you do it in yours, you're always gonna wash out. Just like it says in Zachariah, it's not by your might or power but by his spirit that it's going to get done.

"I knew I could take this old boy, even with a knife, but I came to that point, sink or swim, live or die, Lord, you're gonna do it because I'm tired of doing it in the flesh."

No more had he admitted this than a Worcester police car came up directly behind them.

"Those kind of experiences, they change your life, change the way you live," Tremaine says.

But the frightened and the frustrated were not the only ones touched by the Tremaines. Every morning, above the Spanish grill across from the church, you see an old woman reading her paper and smoking a cigarette. Never anything else.

Hundreds of other elderly people—isolated, lonely, bored—live in a 10-block radius of the church.

"They do run the extremes," Bob says. "We have some of the most gracious, lovely elderly people you could ever meet.

"They're there [in the apartments] simply because financially they can't swing anything else. A lot of them are just as

delicate and dignified as they can be. Then we've got the other extreme. You've got a lot of flipped-out people."

He thinks those in the high-rise may be better off—they do get some company. "It's better than being isolated in these one-room things."

In a sermon one winter, Bob preached that an inner city high-rise was like a prison without bars. Steep hills, snow and ice that might slow the casual traveler loom as unsurmountable obstacles to an elderly person.

continued on page 178

If Bob had waited for Worcester to come
to the redstone church building, nothing much
might have happened. Instead, he reached out
to Worcester. He started by meeting people
where they were—on the street. It was
an eye-opening new culture. "You start walking
around and you always find somebody who needs help."

The coffeehouse and crisis center
grew out of Tremaine's conviction that
"If you've got a building, you ought
to use it any way it can be used.
I'd like to see the church building open
and occupied 24 hours a day."

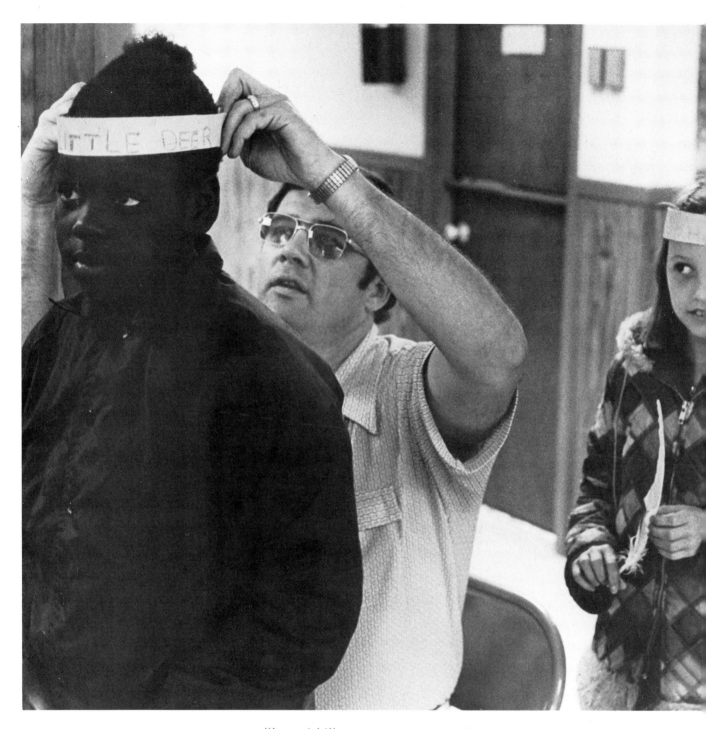

"I would like to see more one-to-one
relationships, which means you've got
to involve more of your people
in different kinds of ministry.
To me, that's when it's really worthwhile."

"I think it's important for a church to minister *with* a community, not *to* a community. It's more open that way, instead of coming as a benevolent big daddy."

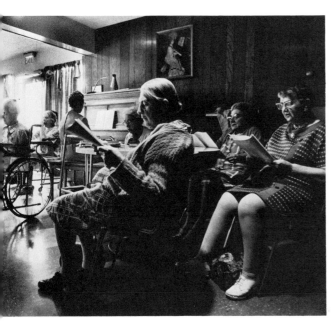

"I think the pastor needs to come
to the place of trusting his laypeople.
Instead of my teaching five Bible
studies and my getting the blessing,
there are five other people teaching
and they're getting the blessing."

The move to a new planned city in Florida brought
a needed change in climate that bettered the Tremaine
family's health. The pace is relaxed here, more
informal and free. Golf carts go from family garage
to first tee; tans and tennis are a style of life.

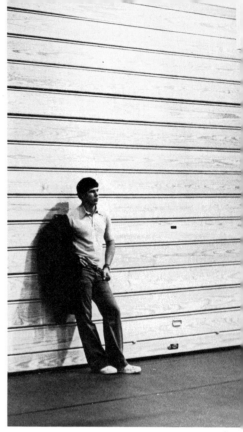

JESUS CHRIST IS LO

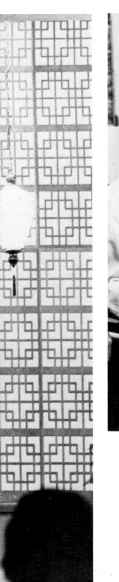

Bob holds services in Palm Coast's yacht club on Sundays, and Bible study on Thursday nights. But he and Glenda have also gotten involved in the Bunnell church, 23 miles away, in the town where their children go to school.

"I used to be a very work-oriented minister.
In New Mexico, man I worked . . . stayed up
two nights a week all night long. But I
just don't do that anymore. I believe
a minister's first obligation is to his family.
When Tim's playing ball, I'm going to be there,
just arrange my schedule so I can.
It's the same with Tori and the little one."

"If you come just up here to the store, you're gonna have to come up this hill and you're gonna have to come down it," Bob says. "Many is the day I have helped a person who has fallen."

Seven years ago, Bob and others started picking up 12 to 40 people every Wednesday and taking them shopping.

"This got started when I was meeting with some other ministers on Main Street. About a dozen ladies would come to the Presbyterian church where we were meeting and somebody would take them shopping. One Wednesday they didn't have anybody, so I drove them and we kept on doing it."

Finally the ladies themselves said, "Look, these folks don't care anything about us, why should you go to their church to pick us up, we'll just go over to your church." The white van now stops at three highrises close to the church, plus a nursing home.

Whenever the housing authority of Worcester got criticism because it isolated elderly people in the inner city, the housing authority has always been able to point to the church and say, 'Oh, they can get anywhere because those folks over at the church will take them wherever they want to go.'"

And it's true.

Tremaine has worked closely with the housing authority. When an older church member who lived alone called him, complaining about vandals, Bob told her to check on a place in the high-rise.

She did. In the meantime, Bob also called his friend at the housing authority. "This member of my church is being harassed by vandals," he said. "Can you get her moved in a hurry?"

Two weeks later, the woman called Bob, asking help to take down her curtains because she was moving.

On several occasions, in four different buildings, the Tremaines would have coffeeklatches, "getting the people together because the housing authority was having difficulty with racial and social problems. We'd let the people fuss and get their aggressions out verbally and then . . . if you could take people screaming and cussing for an hour . . . things would kind of calm down," Bob grins. "We'd also let them deal with the prob-

lems they were having with the housing authority and the people who owned the property, and try to be a mediator.

"It would take sometimes two months to get down where you could talk about what the real issues were."

In addition to coffeeklatches and shopping trips, the church also has delivered surplus food.

"Elderly people couldn't get it because most of them didn't have cars. Cabs wouldn't go down there because they didn't want to hassle with the food either," Bob explains.

So every Monday church members pick up between 13-40 orders of surplus food and deliver it to elderly people who could not get it otherwise. "Now we're plugging into the food stamp thing," Bob says, "because a lot of elderly people don't understand it or won't apply for it.

"This is an important thing," Bob goes on. "It just keeps things going. It keeps the church out before the community."

"There are certain ministries we participate in where we do not reach church growth," Glenda Tremaine once wrote. "We have discovered, however, that when we engage in this type of sharing there are always some won to the Lord and then to the church. This ministry is of the attitude of loving without expecting love in return, giving without expecting thanks."

Once in a while, one of the ladies will shake Bob's hand and leave a dollar bill for gas. "They've got a lot of pride, which I like," he says. "They want to feel like they're contributing."

Through evangelism training, members get "that kind of freedom where we can sit down over coffee and talk about what the Lord is doing in our lives."

This same sense of pride permeates the meal program, started by Bob and assistant Carl Holden.

It is a matter of personal pride for the elderly people to pay 50c even though it's a $2.00 meal.

"Because of our involvement with other things, people come to us with ideas," says Bob. "That's basically the way the meal program got started.

The first meal, 35 people came. Now 70 or more show up to eat and talk.

People serving the meal are volunteers from the community. That fits in with Bob's principle of ministering "with" the community rather than "to" it. "That man Edward over there," he points out. "The ladies call him the milk man because he passes out milk. He is a retired man who thinks it's a good thing to help with this. It gives him something to do and a sense of worth."

The persons touched by the church — through whatever program or person — begin to think of it as their church, whether or not they are members.

On one Wednesday shopping trip, an older woman ventured close to Bob, where others could not hear, and whispered, "Would it be all right for me to put your name on my emergency card as the person to contact from the church?"

When Bob said yes, she then murmured, "Could I put it in my will for you to preach my funeral?"

"This lady is from a Congregational fellowship," Bob explains, "and as far as membership goes, her ties are to the old church where she and her husband went. But she comes every Sunday to our church. As far as I'm concerned, she's a member of our fellowship.

"Our church has voted that if a person is a born again believer and if they have been scripturally baptized, they are invited to join in our communion service, so they do."

Because of the church's community ministries, the number attending worship services and Bible studies has jumped.

Tremaine usually preaches to about 150-200. But it's not rare to have more in weekday Bible studies than in Sunday School.

In 1969 the Tremaines started pushing home Bible fellowships and developed the "search for faith" program.

They'll mail about 400 letters to nearby residents, telling them a Bible study is being started. "Then we call them, telling them again." If they're interested, church members try to visit them and take a *Good News for Modern Man*. Bible study begins on Wednesday, Thursday and Friday.

At one Bible study, nobody came the first night. The second night, one young woman and her husband's grandmother came. The next night they returned, bringing the young woman's husband. Her husband made a profession of faith.

"That was two years ago," Bob says. "Now he's one of our trustees and she's our church treasurer. The Bible study has continued and in that same town we have five Bible studies."

Last spring, the church had 18 Bible studies in 8 towns. Bob used to teach five studies a week. "I was doing five preparations, plus preaching twice. That was just too much."

Now the groups are all being taught by laypersons. Bob has put together *Appropriate Home Fellowship Materials*, and every leader gets that booklet, plus training. "I think the pastor needs to come to the place of trusting his laypeople," Bob says. "We let them have the responsibility for other things than taking the blooming offering on Sunday morning.

"I think we need to permit one another to fail and not be so dad-gummed ego struck we can't fail," Bob says.

"Edison had a thousand different experiments; he wasn't discouraged by that. He said I know a thousand ways it won't work and that's a good thing to know."

In one of the Bible studies Bob tried to start, one man said, "I'm tired of you talking about the Bible, let's just get rid of it." And he threw it on the coffeetable.

Bob kept on talking about God. Then another person interrupted, "I'm so tired of you mentioning the word God, I don't want to ever hear it."

Another chimed in "Well, just spell it backward."

"From where I come from," Bob says, "for somebody to call God dog, that was pretty heavy.

"But I believe we have to start with

Bible study in people's homes is "the best thing we've got going for us right now."

people where they are and that dude, that's exactly where he is.

"I just kept talking. When I approached it from the concept and theory of religion, they said, 'Yeah, that might be interesting.'

"So I said, 'Well, we're going to need some textbooks. What are we going to use?' And the same boy who threw the Bible on the table earlier picked it up and said, 'Well, we might check into this.'

"That's why I like home fellowships, because they can meet any kind of need, anyplace, anytime. You're studying his word and he promises he'll bless you.

"This is another little quirk of mine," he says. "I think Christianity needs to get de-culturized.

What you see up here is an evidence of Christianity in New England; that's where it first became evident to me that I didn't distinguish between Christianity and culture. I came up here and saw other people who were claiming to be Christian and watched things they were involved in and said holy cow, that's not Christianity. Then I began to look at my own stuff, too, and that's not Christianity. This is what my culture says is right rather than what the Bible says is right.

"Like beginning the different organizations, let's take something like deacons.

"We don't have any deacons in our church. Now I believe that's scriptural. When the early church got started they didn't have deacons." But when Bob's church eventually does need deacons, then they'll get them.

"Just because we say we belong to a Baptist church, we've got to have all these things — they don't necessarily meet the needs in every place."

Bob adapted again and again, learning, changing in ways large and small.

He and Glenda faced their most traumatic change — one that eventually led to their move to Florida — when 12-year-old Tori developed leukemia, and 3-year-old Tara fought allergies.

In August, 1974, the Tremaines moved to Palm Coast, a planned community 35 miles north of Daytona Beach. Although no one has been appointed yet to replace the Tremaines in Worcester, those ministries are continuing.

"I was personally anxious to get to

Florida because of what it would do for our family," Bob says. "It's been better than I even really hoped for because we had just had seven years of bad health. Tim was in casts for both feet; Glenda had mastoid trouble and mono. And Torin has leukemia. Winters raked Tara over the coals, she couldn't eat anything.

"When you are so involved in working with your family it really restricted the time I had to do what I was supposed to do," he goes on.

Now Bob says he is rested for the first time in seven years. Since the Tremaines have been in Florida, Tim's playing football, Glenda and Bob play tennis and golf, and Tori is going crabbing and fishing.

"Her whole attitude is much brighter," Bob says. "And all those things they said our baby couldn't eat, she's eating them. That's just changed the whole atmosphere with our family, too, because now you can go to bed and sleep. We hadn't been able to do that for two years."

And, Bob readily admits, he likes living in Florida because he enjoys being in on the start of something new. Palm Coast is one of the largest planned communities in the U.S., with more than 100,000 acres and a projected population of 750,000.

Only about 850 people live here now, though. Bob's job is to start a Baptist mission among them.

Florida Baptist Convention bought 10 acres on one of Palm Coast's main streets, near the St. Joe Canal. But the canal is just a dirty ditch now, and a building is years away. Bob arranged for his group to meet in the yacht club. The Baptists are sandwiched between Catholic services and lunch.

"I like this situation where you do not have a building to operate out of," he says.

Three-year-old Tara, thriving in Florida's sunny weather, sleeps all night, eats "all those things they said she couldn't eat."

"You just go and see what the Lord's gonna call out. You're forced to do things differently from what the normal church is used to doing."

Because the group is allowed only 45 minutes on Sunday mornings, the service must go "bang-bang-bang. That can't amount to much more than a pep rally," Bob says. So he started a Thursday night Bible study, which rotates to different homes.

"We're just learning how to relate to each other and talk the same language. We've got a mish-mash of backgrounds."

One family is from a traditional Southern Baptist background; another is from an independent Bible church in the North. One woman is from an American Baptist church, a man is from a Pentecostal background. "I think that all has got to be molded into a fellowship. We need to understand and relate to each other on a spiritual basis.

"As we develop that, then people will come together and they will see a fellowship within us and a unity within us. You just can't love one another unless you learn how to communicate with one another. You can say you do but that's a bunch of bull."

Bob thinks the Bible study approach in people's homes is "the best thing we've got going for us right now where you can really deal with where people are." The group now is studying 10 lessons on its position in Christ. "We are still on roman numeral 1, arabic number 4. It's good. They just don't miss."

This year, the Tremaines plan an outreach Bible study to reach non-Christians. "We're going to train the people who are coming to the regular Bible study to teach them," Bob says.

About 30 people attend services in the yacht club now; Bob anticipates getting up to 50 this year.

But a lot depends on what happens in the town of Palm Coast. "The economy and inflation is affecting it. Their projection at this point was to have 6,000 people here. We have less than a sixth of that.

"Living out here is just like living in the army—you just hear rumors every day," Bob smiles. "Day before yesterday I heard that all they'd do is have a skeleton crew to keep operating what's operating now and let the other folks move in when it's time for them to move in. Always rumors."

Most of the people who have moved to Palm Coast are middle class, and most are from the North. Bob's neighbors are from New York and Pennsylvania, for instance. But not all of them are retired or old, though many are settled in their lifestyles.

"Many of the people who have moved down here are extremely self-centered," Bob observes. "They don't want to be bothered. The only thing they'll go to is civic association meetings, so they can bitch about the way things are going.

"I think the main difference here in comparison with Worcester is money. Most of the people here do have some kind of money."

People who move to Palm Coast move with some purpose in mind—many are looking for fun, sun and no responsibilities.

"One man, he thought he was going to play golf everyday and just really have a bang-up whoopee time. But after nine months of golf everyday, he's suddenly realized there's got to be more than this.

"I think the longer some of these people are here, the lonelier they're going to get. I think there is going to be a lot of room for a church that will minister."

Bob and Glenda Tremaine want to help grow that church. Services in the yacht club and a Thursday night Bible study are a start. And if Bob can take difficult situations in New Mexico and Massachusetts, and turn them into showcases, he probably can succeed in Florida as well. But sheer energy and enthusiasm won't do it.

In a new situation, with the continuing uncertainty and pain of the family's health, the Tremaines will be relying on something else. Call it dedication, call it courage—it will help this family adapt to yet another new set of circumstances. •

The Tremaines— healthier, more relaxed—plug into a new ministry in a new town.

STEPPINGSTONES
into a
Bold Tomorrow

The intensive exploration of this age will be inner space. New and old methods will be used to discover the mystery of who we are and how we got this way. Many will search for those forces, spirits or otherwise, that dwell within the depths of that inner universe.

Strong efforts will be expended to tap the power of the mind so hauntingly promised if only the right key can be discovered.

Already the adventurous, the discontented and the innovators lead the way into meditation, mind expansion, glossolalia, spiritualism, transactional analysis, inward journeys, spiritual renewal, satanism, mystical religions, astrology, ESP experiments, deep silence, the spirit-filled life and encounter groups. The list becomes endless, and each category breaks down into scores of streams feeding the larger river.

This interest about introspection is but one of the trends affecting national missions. Within this shifting matrix, mission personnel adjust and react, creating minor trends of their own.

How do trends emerge?

What determines the direction in which any group or institution moves? Exploring these questions will help us see the place of national missions within our society.

Three rather broadly defined factors determine the direction: first, what the leaders desire; second, what the followers want; and third, the direction in which the larger society is generally moving.

Leaders are those who best articulate the goals for the group, who initiate the most actions toward attaining those goals, who motivate others to play their roles, who are best able to analyze problem situations to get insight, and *who stimulate the group to do what they already wish to do.*

All leadership depends on followship. No one leads unless someone is willing to follow. A leader's influence derives from the acceptance given him by the followers. When he exercises his leadership in a direction the followers do not want to go, then he loses a degree of influence. Some leaders are so cautious they never risk their influence, yet others sacrifice theirs in a single impetuous act.

Leaders seldom have difficulty leading toward a goal already articulated and accepted by the group. The difficult task is to change a group's direction.

The second factor, the direction in which followers want to move, is determined by tradition, values, self-perception, openness to change, how much change how soon, how much recent change, self-preservation and the pressures of society for adaptation.

The third factor, the direction in which the larger society is moving, will affect the direction of the group either positively or negatively. World conditions, economic health, the influence of mass communications, the population's mobility, current crises, and the perceived crises of the future (such as war and famine) — all these bear upon any large group's direction.

Rapid growth or significant changes in direction occur when all three factors mix to contribute toward a common direction.

For example, such a time came in the 1950s for Southern Baptists to provide a period of exceptional church growth. The housing boom after World War II cared for the population growth and caught up on the lull in housing starts. Vast new suburbs were created everywhere.

Southern Baptists had exploded out of the southern states during the war. In the newer areas, they were asking for churches like the ones they had known in the South. Leaders enunciated the 30,000 Movement, which coincided with the Pioneer Movement. The result was national expansion and church growth in the older states as well as in the ones newer to Southern Baptist work.

Television was born in the '50s, and by the '60s we had a new view of the nation. The national conditions of poverty, discrimination and other complex social ills were seen as though for the first time.

National leaders responded to the crises, and so did many denominations, including Southern Baptists. The SBC at Houston adopted the "Crisis in Our Nation" statement and asked the Home Mission Board to provide leadership for implementation. However, in this case, leaders, followers and society did not always go in the same direction. There was tension among the three, and strong disagreement about the validity of the direction. Nevertheless, the tension was healthy enough to bring significant change. Thousands of churches and individuals led in making one of the major shifts of history in how Southern Baptist churches relate to their communities and to persons in need.

In the late 1960s and early 1970s the drug subculture highlighted the search for meaning that characterizes modern, technological man. The age of introspection — inner space — was born. Not only did the Jesus movement surface, but the search took on bizarre directions into the occult and mystical religions. Society's direction was toward self understanding.

Denominational leaders have responded with a new evangelism emphasis for a Convention which has always seen itself as evangelistic. Thus the current ground swell for evangelism appears to find a convergence of three factors: leaders, followers and society. Whether or not society is passing up Christianity in favor of the mystical, new eclectic religions, or faith in psychology remains to be seen.

An examination of the reasons for the introspective mood reveals a complex mix.

The exploration of outer space turned up few immediate implications for the average person. Once humanity got beyond the gravitational pull of the earth, the mystery of space disappeared. However, the mystery of inner space remains and every person can don the space suit of meditation and soar into this universe.

Technology in our society moved to answer many of our questions about life and the larger universe. Much of the older mystery (like what causes thunder and lightning) was disappearing. We seemingly need mystery, and so we explore or even create the mysterious.

Technology creates more efficient ways for persons to communicate and to perceive the world. We not only find it easier to move to new places, but events of interest are immediately brought to us. Means of mass communications may be more efficient and faster, but they create new voids and needs as we reduce our face-to-face involvement. Emotional hungers will be fed, one way or another.

The awareness made possible by television and other technology also has had a depressing effect as we discovered the complexity of our problems. Tremendous, sudden efforts at correcting poverty or discrimination, establishing peace or eliminating corruption appeared to fail. No sudden panaceas worked.

On top of that, new crises mounted. Each day's telecast told of a new problem, and these began to compound each other. No sudden solutions, however longed for, appeared. Most of us turned away to the entertainment of television, sports or that opening new universe — inner space. Introspection so viewed was unhealthy escapism from a complex world.

Some say society is out of control. The technology that we created to serve us has come to dominate and now threatens to destroy us. The institutions we founded to express the popular will have come to manipulate public opinion and exploit public anxieties.

Others say that people are simply exhausted, having been knocked and dragged by too many forces and appeals.

All of this has contributed to a longing for simpler days, a nostalgia for the past. The '50s, when the post World War II boom provided hope for everyone, look like golden years in comparison.

Meanwhile, what changes were taking place within the national missions effort of Southern Baptists? How were we adjusting and reacting?

No change at the national level of missions for Southern Baptists is as profound as the emphasis upon developing a uniform mission program throughout the nation and the consequent emergence of a national mission strategy.

The raw materials with which to build such a strategy have always been a part of missions.

To see a missionary on the border between Texas and Mexico, or workers within the inner city of Watts or Worcester, Massachusetts, or persons crisscrossing the Northern Plains or struggling with the isolation and needs of Appalachia, is to see the human touch of the national strategy. Its aim is the making of disciples of all persons within the United States.

Behind those missionaries stand years of planning, working agreements between state and national leaders, the setting of priorities for the best use of funds in relation to needs, and the rallying of all Southern Baptists toward common goals.

Some complain that they cannot distinguish between home and state missions. Such a complaint is accurate but not valid, because there is no difference today. The HMB has entered into cooperative state agreements where most mission personnel are jointly employed by the national and the state mission organizations. They are paid on a percentage agreement from each, ranging according to the state's ability to pay. Thus Mike Mojica is employed by the Texas convention and by the Home Mission Board, Henry Chiles by the Northern Plains convention and the HMB. Texas pays probably 80 percent of Mojica's salary, and the reverse is true with Chiles' salary.

In each case and with all the others mentioned in this book (except Glenn Igleheart, who has regional responsibilities) the missionaries are both state and HMB employees. The supervision of the personnel is through the state. The principle governing this is that personnel should be supervised by those closest to them, those who best understand the situation and who relate on a day-by-day basis.

Another trend paralleling this has been the emphasis by the mission agency on upgrading all missionary personnel. Qualifications for career missionary appointment (usually college and seminary degrees and experience) are higher today than at any other time in the history of the Home Mission Board.

As the national board shifted from supervising the mission force, it turned more toward the enlistment and screening of qualified personnel, providing more and more planning for the national mission strategy. It strengthened ways for the equipping of the mission force through study, training and communications.

Another trend, especially apparent in Christian social ministries, reversed the emphasis upon institutions. As funds were directed toward better qualified and better paid missionaries, fewer centers were built and older ones were discontinued.

This did not mean there were fewer buildings in which missionaries worked. Southern Baptists suddenly seemed to discover that there were large church buildings near every center or near where centers were needed. The emphasis shifted to enlisting churches to provide the services once provided by the centers; in most cases, the churches can do a better job. Sid Smith in Watts proves this point. Some centers are still needed, where churches do not have adequate facilities. That is the case of the new center where Freeda Harris conducts her ministry in Appalachia.

Meanwhile, a new line appeared on the job description of most missionaries: "to enlist and to equip others." The single word that described this was "catalyst."

The realization came that no agency could employ enough missionaries, that even the missionaries could not be as effective as laypersons within given situations. Thousands of volunteers were waiting to be given meaningful mission work. Shorter working hours, increased mobility and affluence had multiplied the available volunteers.

Mission planning shifted to take this into account, and missionaries changed from doers to equippers. Persons like Glenn Harada and Mike Mojica discover the needs, match the resources of the Baptist community with those needs, and where necessary they begin the initial work. But soon they pull back and stand alongside the laity or other professionals.

The response of thousands of volunteers for national missions, for service within and without their communities, has to be one of the most hopeful signs on today's horizon. This significant volunteer trend converges with another important trend—the emphasis upon the missionary's role as an equipper, facilitator and catalyst. The trends have their counterpart within the church, as pastors grasp the vision of equipping their members for their ministry in the world.

Societal changes have not only made the ministry of the laity much more possible, they have also made it necessary.

If we haven't already, we will be hearing quite a lot about catalysis. The word comes from the chemistry lab, but it has meanings for human relations.

Catalysis is an action between persons or things, precipitated by a separate agent, usually one that is essentially unaltered by the reaction. In mission areas we are not too concerned if the reaction alters the agent. The emphasis is on having the catalyst cause the action.

The term captures the mission concern to awaken, train and involve thousands of laypersons in doing the work of missions. The missionary not only is multiplied, but the work is usually better done. It is more accepted by those involved in mission efforts, such as the lay pastors with the Navajo Indians.

The shift to the catalytic ministry picked up impetus a few years back when SBC national expansion doubled the land area and tripled the number of people for whom we Southern Baptists felt responsible. There was no way employed missionaries could do all the work. Also we were failing at some difficult tasks — at least not succeeding as well as we would like — when we were unable to cross racial, cultural and language barriers. Missionaries like those in this book enlisted, trained and encouraged persons within those situations to cross the barriers. The results far exceeded previous years.

Today most of those in national missions see their part in determining the needs of the nation, in communicating those needs so others will share the responsibility, in enlisting the laity in accomplishing the task, in equipping laypersons for effective ministry and in putting it all together within a national missions effort. The day of the lay volunteer is here, and mission work is much the better for it.

Until recently, "to make disciples of all persons" had not been a realistic goal for Southern Baptists. For many years the Convention was confined to mostly southern states. But today churches are in every state. For many years Southern Baptist churches were not open to all races. Today ethnic minorities are represented in our churches, in our elected offices, and in the leaders who direct our mission work. A new posture reflects acceptance of all persons, in principle, if not yet in fact, everywhere.

There is another dimension, a geographic or situational one, to the trend to reach all persons. Through the institutional and military chaplaincy, efforts are made to reach persons who are beyond the normal services of the churches — those in prisons, hospitals, mental institutions, industry and the military. A new emphasis has come, no longer expecting all persons to come to the church buildings. One of the most dramatic forms of this emphasis has been resort missions with missionaries, special drama and musical teams, and a larger number of students and Christian Service Corps volunteers going to the beaches, ski slopes, lakes and parks.

A new openness to other Christians and other religions has arisen, seen in this book through the ministry of Glenn Igleheart. Southern Baptists once hid behind the wall of provincialism and acknowledged other groups by our potshots at their beliefs and actions.

But in 1974 we sent the only press representative from a Protestant religious group to the Vatican Council in Rome in the person of Brownlow Hastings of the Department of Interfaith Witness. We established the first Christian-Muslim dialogue in the nation. We held talks among Baptists, Jews and Roman Catholics. Such give-and-take provides us with an understanding of others, breaking the stereotypes, and aiding us in a clearer statement of our own beliefs and practices.

In conversation with the world and with others, we not only must change the form of the message, modernize our language, adjust our vocabulary and change the setting, but those we talk to must share in the shaping of the proclamation. Those of us in communications stress the fact that the receiver is the most important part of the communications process and that the process is not complete until there has been feedback. Too long we have engaged in one-way communication, with little adaptation of the message to what the receiver is hearing.

God's sending of Christ into the world was the supreme example of adapting to the receiver. Christ took on the form of man. M. de Jonge says, "Form and content are not to be separated, because only in genuine communication with the other person can there be proclamation at all."

— Walker Knight

Index

Photograph Identifications

Date Due

BROADMAN
B P
SUPPLIES

266.61
CLASS

318
ACC

Selcraig
(LAST NAME OF AUTHOR)

The Human Touch
(BOOK TITLE)

DATE DUE	ISSUED TO

266.61
CLASS

318
ACC.

Furlow, Elaine Selcraig
(LAST NAME OF AUTHOR)

The Human Touch
(BOOK TITLE)

BROADMAN
B P
SUPPLIES

CODE 4386-03 BROADMAN SUPPLIES
CLS-3 MADE IN U. S. A.